Authors

Vasyl Marchuk
Vasyl Melnychuk

SPECTRUM SLOVAKIA Series
Volume 46

European Integration and Reform of Decentralization in Ukraine during Martial Law

Political Accents

PETER LANG   VEDA

Bibliographic Information published by the Deutsche Nationalbibliothek
The Deutsche Nationalbibliothek lists this publication in the Deutsche Nationalbibliografie; detailed bibliographic data is available in the internet at http://dnb.d-nb.de.

Authors: Vasyl MARCHUK
             Vasyl MELNYCHUK

Reviewers: Prof. Orest KRASIVSKY, Doctor (PhD hab.),
             Adam Mickiewicz University in Poznań (Poland)
             Prof. Yurii OSTAPETS, Doctor (PhD hab.),
             Uzhhorod National University (Ukraine),
             Prof. Anatoliy ROMANYUK, Doctor (PhD hab.),
             Head of the Department of Political Science,
             Ivan Franko Lviv National University (Ukraine)

ISSN 2195-1845
ISBN 978-3-631-91466-3   ISBN 978-80-224-2051-8
ePDF 978-3-631-91467-0
ePub 978-3-631-91468-7
DOI 10.3726/b21552

www.peterlang.com   www.veda.sav.sk

Contents

Introduction

Ukraine's aspiration to European civilization and universal human values is dictated by the entire history of its development, mutual relations with European nations and democratic states. The European integration of Ukraine brought enormous changes in all spheres of life. It had an impact on the internal and external processes of Ukrainian society. This was especially evident with the beginning of the undeclared and unprovoked war of the Russian Federation against Ukraine. In the course of the war, along with security problems, the issue of reforming local self-government became even more acute. Decentralization in Ukraine, which has been going on since 2014, was finally recognized as successful. The internal factor of the modernization of local self-government is the process of decentralization, It covers all levels of the exercise of power and civil initiatives, creating a window of opportunity for local communities to directly influence the development and well-being of their communities.

The experience of the countries of the European Union, which received their status, in particular, by implementing changes in regional self-government, is important for studying and adapting to the needs of Ukraine. The authors depart from the stereotype that everything European by default is necessary for integration into the Ukrainian political system. The study articulates the expediency of paying attention to the cases of those states that, having common features of historical development with Ukraine, more successfully and quickly fulfilled the conditions of EU membership. Such, for example, are the countries of the Visegrad Group. Some of the mentioned problems were covered by the authors in the publications of previous years.[1,2,3,4]

The research updates aspects of the functioning of territorial communities, which lead to a rethinking of the content of their

---

1 Vasyl Marchuk. Ukraine's European Integration in the Political Dimension of Central and Eastern Europe. Trnava: Akademia, 2022. 95 p.

2 Марчук В., Мельничук В. Стан інтеграції європейського досвіду у функціонування системи місцевого самоврядування України. *Регіональні студії*. 2022. №31. С. 34–39.

3 Vasyl Marchuk, Vasyl Dudkevych. European Integration of Ukraine: Political and Security Practices.Trnava: Akademia, 2022. 144 p.

4 Марчук В., Гладій В. Моделі місцевого самоврядування: європейський досвід і реалії України. Вісник Прикарпатського університету. Серія «Політологія». 2020. № 14. С. 215–223.

capacity in peacetime and wartime conditions. Recognizing the importance of the financial component for the united territorial communities in the transitional period of approval of the decentralization reform, the ability to carry out strategic planning of one's own development and to develop new areas of activity was emphasized. In particular, international cooperation at the level of territorial communities strengthens the functional subjectivity of local self-governments and also helps them attract additional donor funding through inter-institutional communication of effective self-government practices. As a persuasive argument, we refer to the experience during martial law of deepening ties with partner cities to supplement cultural and educational cooperation with humanitarian, and financial and material targeted assistance.

Of course, it is impossible to complete such deep and systemic transformations in the state in a short time, but it is quite possible to carry out qualitative monitoring of the potential of socio-political relations, the level of institutionalization of local self-government and the current compliance of self-governing institutions with the requirements of the European integration process. The mobilization of personnel, organizational, and material and technical resources of local self-governments for prompt response to martial law challenges is especially in demand. In the new status and with expanded powers, territorial communities should become reliable partners of the central authorities in ensuring proper resistance to the enemy, protecting the civilian population, and supporting vital economic sectors.

PART 1

Genesis and Retrospective Analysis of Forms of Administrative Transfer of Authority and Decentralization of Power

Although decentralization is one of the leading systemic processes in modern politics, its historical roots go back to the beginning of the 17th century when formulating the postulates of federalism, Western researchers justified their points of view with centrist arguments. The first place here belongs to the German jurist Johannes Althusius, who developed the theory of "popular sovereignty" and predicted the existence of a political association based on primary civil communities. According to the scientist, they were characterized by common consent and pluralism in the use of coercion and force. Two hundred years later, decentralization aspects entered the concept of socialism and anarchism of the French philosopher Pierre-Joseph Proudhon. By the way, it was in the middle of the 19th century that the word "decentralization" entered social and political usage – first in the words of the French historian and statesman Alexis de Tocqueville, and later in the work of his compatriot Maurice Block. A. de Tocqueville not only described the administrative value of decentralization but also claimed that it accustoms citizens to freedom and teaches them to use it correctly. The German jurist O. Gierke gives an answer to the question of why a person has the right to self-government in a world of fairly concentrated power, emphasizing the fact that "the local community as a bearer of customary law was formed earlier than the state, which is why it has an independent source of power".[5] Pierre-Joseph Proudhon pointed out that the ideal combination for the development of the human community is an agricultural decentralized federation.

The prominent Ukrainian public and political figure M. Drahomanov put forward the idea of political decentralization in the context of his commitment to the federal system. The historian wrote about the ability of communities to have internal autonomy and independence from other "self-governments" based on common interests and the tendency to collectively solve problems.[6]

Retrospective analysis of the forms of self-government and laying the foundations of territorial authority within a large state entity can be synchronized with the stages of the entire civilizational

---

5 Gierke O. von. Das deutsche Genossenschaftsrecht. Bd. I. Berlin, 1868. 1111 p.
6 Драгоманов М. «Переднє слово до громади» про державну організацію. Київ: Дакор, 2008. 370 с.

development of mankind, starting from antiquity. There, the primary identification of citizens with the polis prevailed over belonging to the state. Despite the clear stratification of society with an emphasis on political rights, the example of Roman municipalities was indicative of the implementation of self-governing community functions.

The importance of such an experience of ancient formations lies, in our opinion, in fixing the origins of local self-government. Borders that represent municipalities or communities are a prototype of modern administrations of self-governing communities. The resolution of local issues was proposed by holding people's assemblies with the participation of the free population, and the permanently active representative bodies were senates and magistracies, which shared organizational and judicial powers among themselves. The evolution of social and political life provided for the established division of the branches of power in the future as a result of which the judiciary was removed from the jurisdiction of local self-government. Thus, the ancient period can be considered the beginning of the countdown to the acquisition of legal subjectivity by a self-governing community and the institutionalization of the directions of its functioning.

The Middle Ages could be called a difficult period for the formation of the institution of local self-government. This is caused, on the one hand, by the decline of ancient cities and, on the other hand, by the growing influence of the state as an institution that focuses on centralization as the only possible tool for exercising power. State formations in Europe united territories that were unable to resist administrative absorption, and only organizationally strong cities could resist it.

Awareness of the European phenomenon of the city as a synthesis of several basic components has become generally accepted in the educational and scientific environment. These include a fortified fortress, a market, its own stable judicial system and developed legal norms, corporatism, and related autonomy and autocephaly – practices of city self-government and self-management. Economically efficient layers of the population (e.g., landowners), capable of self-organization and self-defense, became the components of the process of establishing self-governing functions of urban settlements during the Middle Ages. The cities that were part of the state territories, such as Byzantium, along with the protection and protectorate of the empire, gradually lost the right to independently resolve local issues. Instead, citizens were given the opportunity to appeal to the emperor for the resolution of socially significant disputes. However, one cannot talk about a complete restriction of municipal freedoms in Byzantium. These opportunities resulted in a combination of not only cultural traditions but also a certain political experience in the implementation of local initiatives. In general, the researchers state that the desire for self-government is characteristic of the cities of the self-governing tradition, and the settlements created by the era of European feudalism went through the corresponding processes in a catch-up manner.

Communal revolutions and self-government in Western Europe in the 11th–13th centuries marked the next stage of the formation of centralized local self-government. The evolution of self-governing subjects consisted not only in changing the name to "communes" and the format of the representative body – "magistrate", "electoral council" – but also their acquisition of independence from the central government and from subordination to the feudal lord. One of the reasons for the so-called "communal" movement is the desire of the lords to get the maximum benefit and profit from the cities. So first there was a struggle for economic freedoms, primarily in trade activities, and then for political rights to manage city affairs collegially without the dictates of the feudal lord. The last aspect is important in the context of determining the nature of the struggle of the townspeople – not against the feudal system but rather against the subjects of oppression.

Historians record the facts of a kind of redemption of the privileges of the commune from the lord. The basis for the implementation of the communal revolution should be sought in the financial sphere, that is, in the sources of the formation of urban wealth. It is primarily represented by the cult of trade, the success of which was demonstrated by the settlements of the Mediterranean coast (Venice, Genoa, Marseille, Montpellier, Pisa, etc.). Another option is the interest of the feudal lord in the prosperity of the cities, for which they received a certain amount of freedom but within the framework of preserving the influence of the lord. It may also be about the fact of reaching a compromise between the citizens and the lord regarding the possibility of obtaining a specified list of self-governing functions It is clear that the list of contemporary tools for expanding the rights and freedoms of the commune also includes an open struggle with the monarch or the head of the church. We assume that it was the format of the last scenario that led to the name "communal revolution".

Institutionally, medieval communes were an organizational system headed by a town council that elected mayors (in France) or syndics (in Italy) who managed the town administration. In this way, the "new" cities received a communal organization, which the early medieval cities did not have. The French historian Augustin Thierry wrote about the emergence of city law, and he called the citizens "a new class of free people". At the same time, let us emphasize the conventionality of such an interpretation because it was not about a specific legal system or an established city jurisdiction but rather about the rules of coexistence of different strata within a single urban space.

There are still disputes over whether the period of the communal movement can really be considered revolutionary and whether it marked the beginning of a new era of self-governing rights in European cities. On the one hand, a hierarchy of representative bodies and their officials was introduced; on the other hand, there were no generally accepted rules that would be universally accepted by the population of cities and feudal lords. The need for such rules was extremely important for the further development of the institution of local self-government.

In the absence of opportunities for the formulation of a unified municipal (self-governing) code, statutes, or city charters – "acts of local self-regulation in local self-government" were created. The value of an urban settlement and belonging to it is determined by phrases that have survived to this day in medieval history, namely "Luft in der Städten frei mache", that is, "city air makes you free". According to one of the versions, the roots of the saying come from an unwritten rule that the escape of a slave to the city and hiding there from the lord for a year made it possible to become a free person, or "citizen of the city". Another expression – "Kein Huhn fliegt über die Mauern" (no rooster flies over the city walls) – defines the closedness of the urban community, which has won its right to establish internal rules and regulations.

A factor in the further evolution of medieval cities was the so-cial and political separation of its citizens from other strata of feu-dal society. As a result, feudal city republics appeared, examples of which are functioning in Spain, Italy, Germany and France. There is an assumption that the prototype of a successful self-governing European city was ancient Rome, whose municipal structure and internal functionality were based not only on Italian cities but also on many other European cities. However, as the example of the Italian Venice, Genoa and Pisa shows, they formed their admin-istrative system, focusing on the predominance of a purely local political elite and the expansion of their own trade capacity. It was the protection of the collective interests of citizens, artisans and merchants that led to the need to create a kind of trade union ("Company"). As a result, it turned into a corporate body of city self-government with legal and political rights, headed by elected consuls. It is important to emphasize that, along with the example of its own experience of municipal development, Genoa became the first among Italian cities to adopt a city charter, or a charter of a free city (1143).

Medieval statutes had the form of a law and were acts that es-tablished the fundamental norms of city organization: powers and composition of authorities, forms of guarantees and minority par-ticipation. Such statutory norms arose during the time of the Bar-barossa Empire when the first prototypes of statutes were created in opposition to Roman-imperial norms under the guise of praeter legem and general legal customs.

As noted by the Ukrainian political scientist V. Gladiy, the con-stitution of free self-governing cities took place in different ways. Some of the settlements on the coast of the Mediterranean Sea (Montpellier, Genoa, Pisa, Venice, etc.) made their fortunes from trade with the East and were able to buy all the privileges en-shrined in the charters of freedom. Part of the cities achieved the right of self-government as a result of a compromise, an agree-ment with the real lord. Other cities won their rights and freedoms in an open struggle with the emperor, king or pope.

The codification of city charters was diverse both in terms of scope and content: local rulers swore according to them, and often the provisions of the charters determined the goals and directions of foreign relations. From the 11th century, relevant acts appear in

Italy (Mantua, Ferrara, Pisa, Cremona), France (Saint Omer, Montauban, Cambrai, Arbois), Normandy, Germany (Mainz, Freiburg, Magdeburg) and England (London, Ipswich). These charters legitimized the self-governing system of that time, and the municipal legislation of the German city of Magdeburg gave the start to written law regarding the organization of city life. The Magdeburg law (1188) provided for the functioning of a hierarchy of city self-government with an elected administration and a court. In the 12th–14th centuries, these norms were adopted in 80 European cities, including Ukrainian ones: Lviv, Khust, Kamianets-Podilskyi, Lutsk, Zhytomyr, Kyiv, Kaniv, Vinnytsia. According to the definition of Professor M. Kobyletskyi, three different models of Magdeburg law operated on Ukrainian lands:

-   the first model functioned in Western Ukrainian lands. Magdeburg law began to spread even in the Galicia-Volyn state and was implemented through the mediation of German colonists. The legal system of Western Ukrainian cities was the closest to the system of German, Polish and other European cities;
-   the second model operated in the city of Kyiv and other Ukrainian cities that were part of the Grand Duchy of Lithuania, and later – the Polish-Lithuanian Commonwealth. Here, the leaders of the cities were called "viyts", who exercised administrative and judicial powers;
-   the third model of city self-government functioned in the cities of the Hetmanship. Here, along with the sources of Magdeburg law and the Speculum Saxonum, Lithuanian Statutes, Ukrainian customary law and normative legal acts of the Hetmanship authorities were used.[7]

Another important document is the Great Charter of Freedoms (1215) although it is considered the origin of documented human rights, the supremacy of freedom and law. In the context of the study, we focus on the following norm of the first constitution of England: "[T]he city of London should have all ancient liberties and free customs both on land and on water. In addition, we wish and prefer that all other cities, towns, settlements and ports also have their liberties and customs". The value of this thesis, in our

---

7 Кобилецький М. Магдебурзьке право в Україні. *Wrocławsko-Lwowskie Zeszyty Prawnicze*. 2019. № 10. С. 9–21.

opinion, lies in the first constitutional consolidation of the principles of self-government, which were further consolidated in various editions of the constitutions of European states: in the Grand Duchy of Lithuania (1529), France (1791), the Polish-Lithuanian Commonwealth (1791), Italy (1848), Prussia (1850), etc. It was the spread of the constitutional process that led to the gradual improvement and content of the concept of self-government, which was embodied in the community concept.

The community approach, or the theory of the natural rights of the community, originates from the project of the French local government system (1790). The ideas were concretized by the French researcher J.-H. Touré, setting them out in a report to the National Constituent Assembly of France "On the Reform of Local Self-Government", which talked about "proper public affairs", which by their nature belongs exclusively to local self-government, and "state affairs", which can be delegated by the state to local self-government bodies.

Fixing the essence and nature of the community approach, we note its simplicity: the independence of communities is determined by their origin, which is not connected and not initiated by the state, and the communities themselves as local communities of people arose earlier than state entities. Therefore, they had a natural right to independently manage their own affairs. The function of the state administration is to control that the community does not go beyond its own competences.

The community approach is considered one of the historically formed theories of local self-government, along with which the public theory of self-government, or the theory of free communities (T. Jefferson, G. Ellinek, J. Mill, A. de Tocqueville) developed. Decisive here are the arguments of A. de Tocqueville, who noted in the treatise "Democracy in America": "Community institutes play the same role for establishing independence as primary schools for science. They open the way to freedom for the people and teach them to use this freedom, to enjoy its peaceful character. Without public institutions, a nation may form a free government, but it will never acquire the true spirit of freedom".[8] The

8 Tocqueville, A. d. (2002). Democracy in America. United Kingdom: University of Chicago Press.

three pillars on which American democracy was based, according to the teachings of A. de Tocqueville, are federalism, communal institutions and the specifics of the judiciary. The communal component was responsible for forming the basis of public perception of freedom and its value. A. de Tocqueville's "formula" included something similar to the theses of J.-H. Touré. The main components are the management of the community purely by its own affairs, the formation of local self-governments with the help of electoral procedures carried out by members of the community and non-interference of the state in the sphere of competence of the community.

The study of the philosopher John Stuart Mill who, in his essay "On Liberty", states that "government is both a huge force that affects human souls and a set of measures for the organization of social life" is important.[9] The right of local self-government is an educational tool for encouraging people to look beyond their own needs and recognize the just demands of other people, which in turn prevents the "barbaric arbitrariness" to which human nature is prone. J. Mill is also credited with the general formulation of the principle of subsidiarity because he emphasized the prerogative of resolving local issues exclusively by the local community.

The global purpose of the political institute of local self-government is to form a connecting link between the state and civil society, which implements the management competences (own and delegated) of the local level determined by the state.

The achievement of political science is the unification of various samples of self-governing practices, framed in approaches, models and theories, including:
- according to the method of distribution of power resources – North American, South European and Scandinavian (Northern European) models of local self-government;
- according to the specifics of local government organization: Anglo-American (Anglo-Saxon), continental (French, Romano-Germanic or European), Iberian and Soviet models.

---

9 Mill, J. S. (1867). On Liberty by John Stuart Mill. United Kingdom: Longmans, Green, and Company.

We associate the modern stage of the theoretical design of the local self-government institute within the subject field of the qualification research with the construction of European formats of self-government structures – bodies, competences, limits of authority, etc. One of the approaches, based on the results of a study of the organization of the local self-government system in 17 countries, suggests dividing them into the following models:

- the dominant role of the mayor (Spain, France, Italy, Portugal, Cyprus, Hungary);
- collective leadership (Belgium, the Netherlands, Luxembourg, the Czech Republic);
- committee management (Denmark, Sweden, Latvia);
- representative and managerial (Finland, Ireland).

In fact, even individual states exhibit different models of local self-government. For example, Germany is a country with a significant amount of differences in land constitutions, where four models of local self-government organization are used, in particular: a "strong mayor" who deals with both local issues and the implementation of state powers (French model); "strong magistrate", elected by the assembly of deputies and exercising executive power collegially (North German model); "strong director" the head of the executive power, elected by the communal council, despite the fact that the burgomaster has mainly representative functions (Anglo-Saxon model); "strong council", which is the highest authority of the community, the burgomaster is the head of the council and at the same time the head of the executive power (South German model). This approach is focused on the primary consideration of who is the determining subject in the organization and implementation of local self-government functions.

Aspects of the formation and transformation of ideas and implementation of the concept of local self-government in one way or another are primarily related to the trend of decentralization. As already mentioned, the decentralization of power is the only condition and requirement for the existence of the institution of local self-government.

The scientists (D. Valadao, H. Kaufman, A. Ozmen, D. Trizman, E. Iuliani) distinguish the following types of decentralization:

- political – aims to give citizens or their elected representatives more powers in making political decisions. This type of decentralization is often associated with pluralist politics and representative government, but it can also support democratization by giving citizens or their representatives more influence over policy formulation and implementation;

- administrative – aimed at the redistribution of powers, responsibilities and financial resources for the provision of public services at different levels of power implementation;
- fiscal – a key component of decentralization, because if local governments and private organizations are to effectively perform decentralized functions, they must have a sufficient level of revenues – either locally collected or transferred from the central government – as well as the authority to make spending decisions. It can take different forms: self-financing, joint financing arrangements, expansion of local revenues through taxes, inter-budgetary transfers, authorization of municipal borrowing and mobilization of national or local government resources through loan guarantees, etc.;
- market (economic) – involves two forms: deregulation and privatization.

The processes envisaged by the above types of decentralization are not autonomous but must occur synchronously, ensuring the general decentralization of power in the state. A partial or fragmentary approach to the implementation of system reforms will not provide the proper result and will not meet the goal of forming independent and economically capable territorial units.

The steps of gradual decentralization of power in European states were based on forms of administrative transfer of powers from the center to communities:

- the direct democracy of the ancient polis, which was realized through people's meetings (commissions, ecclesiastics), which, although they did not provide for general participation and had a consultative nature, introduced a mechanism for involving the population in forming the agenda of the city's functioning;
- a compromise transfer of part of the powers of local administration to citizens through agreements with the feudal lord on the example of communes of the mature Middle Ages;
- codification of city charters and regulation of city self-government in the late Middle Ages;

- acquisition by communities of competences that come from the "natural rights of communities" (18th–19th centuries), which we consider to be the origins of functional self-government;
- separation of communal affairs into separate administrative functions, which should be resolved at the local level (19th–beginning of 20th centuries), which we consider a prototype of the modern understanding of the principle of subsidiarity;
- multi-level systems of local self-government with legally established powers and demarcation of influence with central authorities (since the second half of the 20th century).
- The transition from philosophical and theoretical categorization to the actual implementation of the norms of power decentralization in the functioning of political systems and regimes lasted for several hundred years. In the 20th century, the principle of subsidiarity as an approach to decision-making at the level of its direct implementation did not become part of deep democratic transformations in Western states. All this time can be called approbation in terms of the search for justification for moving away from centralized forms of management, development of tools, so that the new practice is implemented by political elites and accepted by society.

PART 2

**Peculiarities of Local Self-government
Models in European Union Member States**

The reform of the system of local self-government in Ukraine, which is part of a more global process of decentralization of power, involves changes that have already been partially or fully tested in various countries of the European Union. Therefore, the practices of implementing sustainable models of local self-government and the development of national formats within the EU, the challenges that accompanied these processes, and the specifics of the interaction of various political institutions at the central and regional levels are of not only scientific but also purely governmental interest. We would like to point out that sectoral monitoring proves the positive impact of awareness of citizens and communities on the potential and capabilities of local self-governments in new conditions on the effectiveness of the decentralization reform.[10]

For further analysis, it is worth meaningfully grouping EU member states. The study covers the trends in the formation of the system of local self-government in the states that are part of the G7 (Germany, France, Italy), which may have formed permanent models of local self-government; Scandinavian countries (Denmark, Sweden, Finland), where, among others, the geographical factor in the formation of the local self-government system is important; the countries of the Visegrad Group (Poland, the Czech Republic, Hungary, Slovakia) as close to Ukraine in terms of historical development; and Baltic States (Latvia, Lithuania, Estonia), which became an example of successful implementation of decentralization reforms in the context of post-Soviet transformation and active European integration. Of particular importance for Ukraine are those countries that are territorially commensurate; among the selected groups, we emphasize the self-governing practices of France, Sweden and Germany.

EU member states and at the same time members of the G7 France, Italy and Germany long ago formed and implemented the rules of local authorities. For a long time, these rules were not updated, which led to such problems as the imbalance of powers of central and local level, the politicization of the decentralization process, the non-systemic nature of reforms, etc. These problems are mainly in Italy and France. Germany, given its federal struc-

---

10 Самоврядування та децентралізацію вже можна викладати у школі. *Децентралізація*: Офіційний вебпортал. 2020. URL: https://decentralization.gov.ua/news/12853

ture, has mostly avoided such problems. In Germany, local self-government did not become an independent level of the federal system, but as a part of the general political system, it declared itself as a stable and rather flexible institution, where the principle of subsidiarity is functionally applied.

Germany, from the point of view of scientific interest, is a contradictory country: on the one hand, its system of local self-government is quite established, and local political elites often appeal to the experience of its formation; on the other hand, we should not forget about the federal system of Germany, which largely determines the features of self-government of the lands.

Local self-government in Germany belongs to the continental model. In this case, state management bodies (central) and local self-governments (local representative bodies) are combined. Currently, the Constitution of the Federal Republic of Germany states that "the constitutional system of the lands must correspond to the basic principles of a republican, democratic and social legal state in the spirit of the current Basic Law. In lands, districts, and communities, the people must have representation created by general, direct, free, equal, and secret elections" (Article 28).[11] The German model of self-governance provides for three representative levels – states, districts and communities. The Constitution also enshrines the right of communities to decide within the law under their own responsibility on all local matters and the basis of their own financial responsibility, which is ensured by tax revenues in accordance with established tax rates.

Analogies can be drawn with the current system of organizing local self-government in Ukraine, where there are also local representative bodies of various levels, which are endowed with self-governing powers, primarily fiscal ones. However, let's also point out the specificity of German local self-government, which distinguishes it from other European ones. In Germany, several models of local government organization coexisted for a long time: the South German model (Bavaria, Saxony, Baden-Württemberg), the North German model (Lower Saxony, North Rhine-Westphalia), the burgomaster council model (Rhineland-Palatinate, Saarland,

---

11 *Grundgesetz für die Bundesrepublik Deutschland hat am 23. Mai 1949.*URL: http://www.gesetze-im-internet.de/bundesrecht/gg/gesamt.pdf

rural communities of the state of Schleswig-Holstein), council-magistrate model (Hessen, state-city of Hamburg).[12] The key differences in the specified models are the ratio of powers of the council and the burgomaster, the way the council and the corresponding executive committees are formed. Despite the complexity of the system of coexistence of such models, they corresponded to the vision of the population of the type of public power that was most suitable for one or another administrative-territorial unit. At the same time, all municipal entities were legal entities with separate property, an independent budget, the right to enter into legal relations, be a plaintiff and a defendant in court, and act through their own management bodies. In Ukraine, with the entry into force of the norms of the decentralization reform, we can also claim that a similar experience has been approved.

The changes taking place in the system of local self-government in Germany, related to the municipal reform, are similar to the decentralization trends in Ukraine. First, it is about the consolidation of communities, which caused protest movements in East Germany. Second, there is a unification of models of self-government organization in communities with a tendency towards the South German model of management while preserving certain features of the construction and functioning of the system of local self-governments in various federal states. Third, the reform was supposed to increase the efficiency of local administrations and reduce the noticeable demographic imbalance of the eastern and western lands.

The advantage of the German self-government system is the general support of the population for local representative bodies. Citizens associate with them the solution of important issues for communities. As the German researcher T. Wurtenberger notes, "a decentralized state must rely on civil society or contribute to the formation of such civil society. Granting rights to local or regional self-government may prove fruitless if citizens are not willing to take political responsibility at the local or regional levels".[13]

---

12 Kaspar M. *Entwicklungen, Unterschiede und Gemeinsamkeiten der deutschen Kommunalverfassungen.* Universität Konstanz, 2006. URL: https://d-nb.info/1081295880/34
13 Бриль М. (у співавт.). *Успішна територіальна громада: будуємо разом.* Харків: Видавничий будинок Фактор, 2018. 128 с.

The sectoral interaction of Ukraine and Germany in recent years concerns the issues of real demarcation of the powers of the central executive and local self-government levels, increasing the level of financial capacity of communities and forming an open dialogue with local residents in order to improve both information about the reform and the importance of direct participation of the population in the implementation of local initiatives. In particular, these directions were repeatedly voiced at public events by the special envoy of the German government for reforms in the spheres of governance and decentralization in Ukraine G. Milbradt.[14]

The constitutions of Italy (1948) and France (1958 with amendments from 2008) determine the right of territorial units to form their own elected authorities, to exercise the powers provided for by law.[15]

The Italian Constitution also regulates the right to collect local taxes and own material resources (Article 119). Contradictions that accompany the process of transformation of local self-government in Italy and France do not allow this process to be completed. Some call the regionalization trends of Italy a means of resisting manifestations of separatism, while others call them the initial stage of the country's federalization. In this context, it is possible to talk about the strengthening of local autonomy with the introduction of budget decentralization, but at the same time, the center's powers are decreasing at a much slower pace.

For a long time, the system of state and political management of Italy was characterized by a significant amount of state control over local authorities. The gradual departure from these practices began in 1990 with the adoption of the Law on Local Self-Government Reform; the expansion of the financial powers of the regions was legislated in 1995. The Law "On Urgent Measures to Streamline Administrative Activities and Decision-Making and Control Procedures" of 1997 simplified reporting of local authorities and detailed competences of municipal, provincial and regional coun-

---

14 Мільбрадт Г. Україна повинна думати на перспективу. *Укрінформ.* 2019. URL: https://www.ukrinform.ua/rubric-regions/2647503-georg-milbradt-specialnij-predstavnik-uradu-nimeccini.html
15 Концепція розвитку сільських територій від 23.09.2015 р. *Верховна Рада України*: Офіційний вебсайт. URL: https://zakon.rada.gov.ua/laws/show/995-2015-%D1%80#Text

cils.[16] However, this was only the beginning of Italy's path to establishing the principle of decentralization.

The current Italian Constitution regulates local autonomy, stipulating that the Republic consists of municipalities, provinces, metropolitan cities, regions and the center. Municipalities, provinces, capital cities and regions have their own autonomous bodies with their own statutes, powers and functions (Article 114).[17] During 2000–2014, Italian legislation accumulated and adjusted the powers of local authorities at different levels and the format of their implementation. In fact, this process is still going on. Currently, municipalities that have received financial autonomy can carry out the general organization of administrative, financial and accounting management and control, provide social and communal services, engage in urban planning, take care of public safety, etc. The powers of the provinces include issues of territorial planning, provision of transport services, formation of a school network, and control of the labor market. During the period of constitutional reform, the provinces had broader powers, which were limited by the so-called "Del Rio Law" in 2014.[18]

At the current stage of decentralization of power, the Italian model provides for the transfer of functions to lower regional levels in four main directions:
- economic development and production sector;
- territorial planning, environment and infrastructure;
- administrative and communal services.

For Italy, the issue of establishing a dialogue with the regions remains relevant – in particular, in the direction of overcoming the consequences of global crises. For this purpose, the country adopted the National Recovery and Sustainability Plan, the implementation of which aims to ensure stable inclusive economic development, primarily with the involvement of the potential of the regions.

---

16 Colletta C. L'evoluzione storico-legislativa delle autonomie locali: gli Enti Locali nell'ordinamento italiano. *Diritto.it*. 2021. URL: https://www.diritto.it/levoluzione-storico-legislativa-delle-autonomie-locali-gli-enti-locali-nellordinamento-italiano/
17 Конституція Італійської Республіки (з передмовою Володимира Шаповала). Київ: Москаленко О. М., 2018. 62 с.
18 European Charter of Local Self-Government (Strasbourg, 15.10.1985). *Council of Europe Portal*. URL: https://rm.coe.int/european-charter-of-local-self-government-gbr-a6/16808d7b2d

The centralization of power in presidential-parliamentary France presupposes the presence of a central level of management in regional and local levels. Therefore, the lack of decentralization here is partially compensated by the deconcentration of power. And if the scope of powers of local councils is often criticized, the competencies of elected officials (primarily mayors) are gradually increasing, uplifting the influence and recognition of mayors.

For a long time, France has been going through the process of reforming local self-government, which, although it takes place with varying intensity and effectiveness, is always based on the goal of decentralization and deconcentration of power. Currently, we can highlight several historical stages of the search for the optimal self-governing model for France:

1968 – S. de Gaulle's new concept of relations between the state and local government, the essence of which is laid out in the Lyon speech: "General evolution, in fact, leads our country to a new equilibrium. The centuries-old effort of centralization, which for a long time was necessary for our country to achieve and maintain its unity, despite the differences of the provinces that were successively annexed to it, is no longer necessary. On the contrary, it is regional activity that is now the source of tomorrow's economic power".[19] Despite the failure of the 1969 reform, when it was not possible to create self-governing regions, the recognition of the need to increase the powers of the French provinces, primarily to increase their financial independence, marked the beginning of the further institutionalization of decentralization trends;

1981–1983 – adoption of the "Defferre Act". The then Minister of the Interior and the mayor of Marseille G. Defferre proposed to legislate the replacement of strict state control over local affairs with simple administrative and financial supervision, which was proclaimed in the law on the rights and freedoms of municipalities, departments and regions of March 2, 1982. Consequently, the prefects could no longer intervene in the acts of local authorities but only refer them to the administrative court. An administrative

---

19 La loi Defferre sur la décentralisation est promulguée. *Services de la Première ministre.* 2019. URL: https://www.gouvernement.fr/partage/10896-2-mars-1982-la-loi-defferre-sur-la-decentralisation-est-promulguee

judge could decide whether they complied with current legislation. Local executive power passed from the prefect to the heads of elected local councils with increased powers. Already in 1983, a new law changed the distribution of powers between municipalities, departments, regions and the center. Any hierarchy between local authorities was also eliminated. The initial justification for the changes was based on a purely economic calculation: in the revenues of territorial communities, the share of contributions provided by the state was equal to the income from local taxation.[20] This meant that the communities would be able to maintain themselves in the part of powers that relate to local affairs;

1992 – the framework law on the territorial administration of the republic was adopted, which put state services and local authorities on equal terms: "territorial administration of the republic is provided by local authorities and decentralized state services".[21] The law also introduced the principle of subsidiarity. In the same year, the so-called "Deconcentration Charter" was established;

2002–2004 – the principle of decentralization was established constitutionally (Constitutional Law of March 28, 2003). The local government received financial autonomy with a note that its resources must necessarily contain a tax component, the right to hold a local referendum and an additional list of powers (economic development, education, culture, social protection, etc.)[22];

2019 – the start of a new stage of the reform of the territorial organization of the state, which aims to demarcate the powers of the state and local authorities, to reorganize the decentralized net-

---

20 Discours de M. Gaston Defferre, ministre de l'intérieur et de la décentralisation, au congrès des présidents des conseils généraux, sur le projet de loi relatif à la répartition des compétences, Lyon le 23 septembre 1982. *Vie-publique.fr*. URL: https://www.vie-publique.fr/discours/256670-gaston-defferre-23091982-repartition-des-competences
21 La révision constitutionnelle relative à l'organisation décentralisée de la République, acte II de la décentralisation. *Vie-publique.fr*. 2019. URL: https://www.vie-publique.fr/eclairage/38440-lacte-ii-de-la-decentralisation-la-revision-constitutionnelle#l%E2%80%99autonomie-financi%C3%A8re-des-collectivit%C3%A9s-territoriales
22 La révision constitutionnelle relative à l'organisation décentralisée de la République, acte II de la décentralisation. *Vie-publique.fr*. 2019. URL: https://www.vie-publique.fr/eclairage/38440-lacte-ii-de-la-decentralisation-la-revision-constitutionnelle#l%E2%80%99autonomie-financi%C3%A8re-des-collectivit%C3%A9s-territoriales

work of state institutions (in particular, for this purpose, regional administrations of the economy, employment, labor and solidarity were created in 2020).[23]

The experience of France, first of all, focuses on the long-term decentralization process, which is complemented by aspects of power deconcentration, finding a balance between the powers of central authorities, the needs and potential of regions, and democratization of interactions between local self-government bodies. It is significant that democratic state-building was not successfully implemented on the first attempt, requiring lengthy consultations, negotiations and compromises.

Denmark, Sweden and Finland are Scandinavian, or Nordic, countries, which in the context of the construction of the local self-government system are united mainly by geography, because historically and politically, local self-government in these countries has developed differently. The currently valid Danish Constitution of 1953 enshrines "the right of municipalities to independently carry out local affairs (powers) determined by law under state control". The relevant legislation describes the range of fields covered by the competences of Danish self-government bodies, namely: social security services, primary education, employment of the population, environmental protection, health care, interaction with business, etc. We consider certain limitations in the right to levy local taxes to be a significant drawback in the performance of these functions. On the other hand, the country ensured the independence of local self-governments from the government, including among the governors' duties only the verification of the legality of local government actions.

The tradition of local self-government in Finland has been transformed from the constitutionally granted right to provide public services (1919) to the ability to collect and manage local taxes under the control of the Ministry of Finance (1999).[24] The Finnish two-tier system of local self-government is still in the process

---

23 La loi Defferre sur la décentralisation est promulguée. *Services de la Première ministre.* 2019. URL: https://www.gouvernement.fr/partage/10896-2-mars-1982-la-loi-defferre-sur-la-decentralisation-est-promulguee
24 Finland's Constitution of 1999 (with Amendments through 2011). Constituteproject.org. URL: https://www.constituteproject.org/constitution/Finland

of reform. It also concerns the aspects of fiscal decentralization and the transfer of powers, primarily with regard to health care and social services, which currently belong to the competences of the municipal (basic) level. This creates pressure on local finances; therefore, since 2016, the need for a reform that would transfer the specified functions to the level of regions has been discussed.[25] The peculiarity, due to which the experience of Finland was periodically appealed to in the context of Ukrainian realities, concerns its bilingual status. The official languages are Finnish and Swedish (Swedes make up no more than 6 % of the Finnish population). And since 1921, the Åland Islands, where Finnish Swedes live compactly, have the special status of a self-governing, monolingual province. Such asymmetry in legally recorded bilingualism and its actual manifestation is unique but indicative in the context of the preservation of historically formed features at the level of state-building and the implementation of self-government.

The two-level model of local self-government in Sweden was formed in the middle of the 20th century. There are two levels of democratic governance: municipalities (290) and regions (20). Local and regional self-governments have elected bodies – assemblies or councils and administrations that make decisions, but a lot of powers are delegated to the localities.[26] In modern conditions, the Swedish system of territorial organization of power has a wide autonomy in the exercise of local powers, with the right to collect local taxes (their types are determined by the parliament at the request of the government, but about 30 % of personal income taxes are returned to the localities).

The peculiarity of the functioning of local self-government in Sweden is the introduction of a multi-component system of control over its activities. On the part of the central government, it is carried out by sectoral ombudsmen, national councils and agencies, and district administrations, and the public is allowed to exercise control by applying to the district administrative courts. The finan-

25 Finland – unitary state organized on a decentralized basis. *European Committee of the Regions.*2022. URL: https://portal.cor.europa.eu/divisionpowers/Pages/Finland.aspx

26 Шведський погляд на нагляд у місцевому самоврядуванні. *Децентралізація: Офіційний вебпортал.* 2020. URL: https://decentralization.gov.ua/news/12460

cial capacity of local self-governments allows periodic review of the powers of executive bodies in the direction of their transfer to the self-governing level. This leads to the need to review inter-budgetary relations, where the leading task of the state becomes the equalization of the budgetary security of municipalities.

Sweden is characterized by a high level of independence of local self-governments in solving tasks assigned to them by law. State authorities are trying to reduce the scope of their own powers in favor of local self-government bodies. The main responsibility in the spheres of social security, health care, education, and ecology is provided at the level of municipal entities. In these areas, the state carries out general legislative regulation and partially provides financing within the system of state transfers and equalization of the budgetary security of municipal entities.[27]

The experience that is important to articulate for Ukraine is the Swedish attraction to functional and fairly effective cooperation at the level of local self-government. The Swedish Association of Local Authorities and Regions (SALAR) is the largest employers' organization in the country. Its role is to negotiate collective bargaining agreements on behalf of municipalities, counties and regions for more than a million workers (a quarter of the country's total employment). Almost half of these workers are employed in the health and social care sectors, and about a third in the education sector, which covers pre-school, basic and upper secondary education at the municipal level.[28] The Swedish Association of Local Authorities and Regions provides an example of several more useful practices. It forms databases on the activity and efficiency of various sectors of the local economy, interacts with government structures on legislative changes and regions' sensitivity to them and actively cooperates with key supervisory institutions (Chancellor of Justice and Parliamentary Ombudsman). It is about competent advocacy of the interests of local self-government at the level of the central government, as well as constructive interaction of local self-government units.

---

27 Федоренко В., Чернеженко О. Конституційні моделі місцевого самоврядування у державах-учасницях ЄС, Швейцарії та України: монографія. Київ: Ліра-К, 2017. 288 с.
28 Шведський погляд на нагляд у місцевому самоврядуванні. Децентралізація: *Офіційний вебпортал*. 2020. URL: https://decentralization.gov.ua/news/12460

All four countries of the Visegrad Group are unitary, with stably functioning branches of government – a common and simultaneous history of European integration, which was successfully completed in 2004. However, the process of building the system of local self-government in these four states had its own specifics. As Professor V. Klymonchuk notes in his research, the Visegrad Group states are characterized by a "reformist" transition, which involves not only the activity of political elites but also the broad inclusion of various segments of the population in political processes. In addition, the transformation of political systems in Poland, the Czech Republic[29], Slovakia and Hungary was accompanied by a deep reform of the administrative-territorial system, which led to the creation of an effective model of a decentralized state and the establishment of the territorial community as an independent political actor. The administrative-territorial reforms applied by the countries of Central and Eastern Europe after gaining independence and announcing their desire to integrate into the European Union took place in the context of the Western European policy of regional development.[30]

Poland came to the modern three-level model of local self-government from the awareness of the direct connection between the implementation of decentralization, socio-economic liberalization and market reforms. Prolonged discussions regarding the choice between two and three levels of government organization were not only expertly but also scientifically based. Polish academician E. Regulski described the key principles that will guarantetransformae the success of the reforms: the political will of the state leadership, the participation of competent experts, public support and qualified management personnel. However, there was a long period of transformations before such a meaningful approach to ensuring the effective work of local authorities: from the three-level model (voivodships, districts, communities), which operated before the reform of the 1970s, to the two-level structure of local

---

29 In this context, more see Haydanka Y. and M. Martinkovic. *Decentralization and Electoral Processes. Political Fragmentation of the Czech Republic.* Trnava: Akademia, 2022. p. 28–40.

30 Климончук В., Масик Ю. Особливості перетворення політичних систем Балтійських країн у складі ЄС. *Вісник Прикарпатського університету. Серія «Політологія».* 2020. № 14. С. 250–257.

self-government with communes and provinces. Obviously, the authority of these units in the reform agenda was inferior to the issue of their quantitative reduction.

The end of the 1980s and the construction of the Third Polish Republic became decisive for local self-government because communes acquired constitutional subjectivity and received property rights. Having proven the capacity of communities and the new territorial administration, Poland continued to improve the system of local self-government. During 1989–1990, more than 100 laws were amended.[31] Laws regulate the competences and powers of local self-governments regarding finances, assets, and other property, which self-governing subjects have already learned to use productively. Further changes in the organization of public power related to the implementation of European integration practices and only strengthened the factors of decentralization of the country.

The constructive experience of Poland concerns the system algorithm that the country took as a basis. Powers, their scope and mechanisms of implementation are clearly prescribed in the legislation, primarily in the Constitution. Its revision from 1997 and the political will of the newly elected parliament marked the end of an important stage of decentralization of the country, which established a mutually agreed three-level model of local self-government in Poland (voivodships – counties – communes). In general, the constitutional component of the institutional design of local self-government in Poland is quite structured and provides an answer to key questions regarding the organization of the self-government mechanism in the country. Let's focus on several important points:

–   a self-governing community consists of residents of territorial units. Local self-government participates in the exercise of public power, performs tasks assigned to it on its own behalf and under its own responsibility (Article 16). Along with the recognition of the fact of self-government, the Constitution guarantees compliance with this principle through protection in court (Article 165.2), while a similar provision in the Constitution of Ukraine concerns the "rights of local self-government" (Article

---

31 Федоренко В., Чернеженко О. Конституційні моделі місцевого самоврядування у державах-учасницях ЄС, Швейцарії та Україні: монографія. Київ: Ліра-К, 2017. 288 с.

145). Disputes regarding duplication of powers or layering of functions of various institutions in the system of state adminis-tration and local self-government shall be resolved through the arbitration of administrative courts (Article 166.3)[32];

- the financial basis for the implementation of the functions of lo-cal self-governments is formed, in particular, by constitutional articles on the income of territorial self-government units, the right to set local tax rates and fees, the right to property and other property rights (Articles 165, 167, 168);

- the Polish constitution defines the right of a self-governing community to hold a referendum on issues affecting that com-munity, including early termination of the powers of a local self-governing body elected in direct elections (Article 170). The implementation of the specified norm takes place within the framework of the Law on Local Referendum from Septem-ber 15, 2000.[33] The Ukrainian experience, along with the con-stitutional recognition of the possibility of holding local refer-endums by territorial communities, has a gap in the form of the absence of a legally established procedure: the law on the all-Ukrainian referendum was recognized as unconstitutional, and with regard to local ones, there is only a draft law that is currently under consideration by the Verkhovna Rada;

- a unit of territorial self-government in Poland has the right to join international associations of local and regional self-governing communities, as well as to cooperate with local and regional communities of other states (Article 172).[34] This norm is additionally regulated by legislation, but in practice, it refers to effective practices of humanitarian support by communities in regions of other states, as provided for in the settlements of Ukraine affected by the military aggression of the Russian Fed-eration. As for Ukraine, the Constitution does not provide for such competences for local self-government bodies, appealing

---

32 The Constitution of the Republic of Poland(2nd April, 1997). URL: https://www.sejm.gov.pl/prawo/konst/angielski/kon1.htm

33 Ustawa z dnia 15 września 2000 r. o referendum lokalnym. Strona główna Se-jmu Rzeczpospolitej Polskiej. URL: https://sip.lex.pl/akty-prawne/dzu-dziennik-ustaw/referendum-lokalne-16885627

34 The Constitution of the Republic of Poland (2nd April, 1997). URL: https://www.sejm.gov.pl/prawo/konst/angielski/kon1.htm

"in other matters of local self-government organization, formation, activity and responsibility of local self-government bodies"
to the laws (Article 146). The Law "On Local Self-Government"
describes the relevant powers in the field of foreign economic
activity (e.g., ensuring the implementation of Ukraine's international obligations in the relevant territory within the granted
powers) and also establishes the right of local self-governments
to join industry international associations, which is obviously
a variant of opportunities, provided for in Poland.[35]
Regarding Slovakia, it is difficult to determine a conditional
starting point for further changes in the system of local self-government. The old, sentially Soviet model of local self-government
operated in the country until 1998, having neither the influence
of institutional memory nor alternatives during the systemic
transformation of the entire state policy. The key unsolved problem was the ingrained equalization principle in the implementation of the rights of municipalities, regardless of their size, which
in practice meant that a city with a population of 50,000 people
and one with a hundred citizens perform the same tasks. Since
1998, it is possible to trace the growth of territorial autonomy
with the emergence of the second, local level of local self-government, and with it the introduction of the principle of subsidiarity, and the strengthening of activities and initiatives for the
development of cities, villages and towns. In Slovakia, where the
vision of local self-government reform did not gain consensus in
the political class[36], these transformations de facto became a government project when the government approved the Concept of
Decentralization. In a few years, the National Council adopted
the "Project of Decentralization of State Power for 2003–2006".[37]
Since 2004, a three-level model of state administration has been

---

35 Закон України «Про місцеве самоврядування в Україні» від 21.05.1997 р. (зі змінами). *Законодавство України.* URL: https://zakon.rada.gov.ua/laws/show/280/97-
%D0%B2%D1%80#Text
36 In this context, more see Martinkovič M. Coalition Governments and Development of the Party System in Slovakia / Peter Lang GmbH — VEDA, Publishing
House International Academic Publishers of the Slovak Academy of Sciences
Bratislava, 2021, p. 82-97.
37 Decentralizácia verejnej správy 2003–2006. Apríl 2003. URL: https://www.ko-
munal.eu/images/pdf/Projekt_decentralizacie_2003_2006.pdf

formed in the country: local level, regions (higher territorial units), state level (central).

The long-term redistribution of management options between the center and regions, in particular, regarding the provision of administrative services, ended with the transfer of the powers of the government spectrum to the level of municipalities and regions, which almost do not overlap in the implementation of their functions. The purpose of such a step is to improve the quality of administrative services for the population and its self-organized entities. The transfer of a significant amount of government powers to the local level was also accompanied by fiscal decentralization (since 2005). Thanks to it, 70.3 % of personal income tax was transferred to local self-government bodies, 23.5 % was left to the budgets of higher territorial units and only 6.2 % was directed to the state budget.[38] The transfer of powers without an adequate expansion of the financial base will result in the transformation of local self-governments into institutions engaged in the passive implementation of state policy. In the absence of funds, they do not have their own resources for the development of the corresponding administrative-territorial unit, and thus relieve themselves of responsibility for its socio-economic situation.[39]

In the context of the democratization of state power and the country's European integration, Slovakia followed the norms of the European Charter of Local Self-Government, compliance with which is confirmed by monitoring studies of the Council of Europe.[40] The development of the local self-government system is an ongoing process, and now it is focused on solving specific tasks, for example, on the approbation of effective cases of cooperation between municipalities, which is carried out within the framework of European and national projects. Among the most large-scale

---

38 Лондар Л. Напрями реалізації політики децентралізації в умовах розширення прав місцевих органів влади і забезпечення їх фінансової та бюджетної самостійності: аналітична записка. *Національний інститут стратегічних досліджень*. 2016. URL: https://niss.gov.ua/doslidzhennya/ekonomika/napryami-realizacii-politiki-decentralizacii-v-umovakh-rozshirennya-prav

39 Цірнер М., Марадик Н. Особливості фіскальної децентралізації в Словацькій Республіці: досвід для України. *Політичне життя*. 2020. № 2. С. 57–62.

40 Brezovnik B., Hoffman I., Kostrubiec Ja. Local Self-Government in Europe. Institute for Local Self-Government Maribor, 2021. 445 p.

in recent years is the national project of the Association of Slovak Cities "Modernization of Local Territorial Self-Government" (2018–2021). Among the project's priorities there are named:
-   introduction of effective decision-making tools at the local level;
-   implementation of the so-called "joint self-governance" and benchmarking tools;
-   exchange of successful solutions implemented in other municipalities;
-   strengthening the principle of good governance, which means making legal, legitimate, effective and transparent decisions, the consequences of which are known in advance;
-   timely intervention that will increase the awareness of elected representatives and professional workers in the legislative sphere;
-   improving the quality of professional training of personnel in local self-government bodies;
-   creation of conditions for changing the current municipal legislation, as well as improving the effectiveness of control activities in the industry;
-   as a conclusion, a comparative analysis of the local self-government model of Slovakia with the corresponding indicators of the countries of the Visegrad Group will be carried out. This will allow to determine which tools and established solutions will contribute to the modernization of self-government and increase its efficiency.[41]

The beginning of the formation of the state strategy for the modernization of the local self-government system means that the transformation process in Slovakia has been completed. Currently, the issue of fragmentation of the local self-government system and the lack of sufficient political will to unify communities remain unresolved. Existing communities are not always ready for constructive cooperation among themselves, closing within their own jurisdiction. The influence on the situation of the central gov-

---

41 Miestna samospráva bude vedieť reagovať na nové trendy, umožní to operačný program Efektívna verejná správa. *Ministerstvo vnútra SR*. 2018. URL: https://www.minv.sk/?aktuality_zahranicna_pomoc_MV_SR&sprava=miestna-samo-sprava-bude-vediet-reagovat-na-nove-trendy-umozni-to-operacny-program-efek-tivna-verejna-sprava

ernment is minimal, because, guided by the current legislation, the state only exercises control over the observance of constitutional principles. There is a clear similarity to similar processes in Ukraine when the principle of voluntary association of communities was often replaced by the decisions of the center. In both cases – Slovak and Ukrainian – the solution to problematic issues lies in the plane of communication and information: from the center to the communities, from the existing local self-governments to the population.

In the formation of the system of local self-government in the Czech Republic, V. Gladiy singled out five meaningful stages:

1. 1990–1991 – when the Czech Republic abandoned the three-level structure of administrative management of the 1960 model and defined the community as the basic level of local self-government;

2. 1992–1995 – the Czech Republic separated from Slovakia, and adopted its own constitution, which regulates local self-government;

3. 1996–1997 – the Ministr of Regional Development of the Czech Republic was established; the Constitutional Law on the creation of 14 higher territorial units of self-government was adopted, which became the basis of regional policy after the country's accession to the EU;

4. 1998–1999 – the Coordination Committee and the Agency for Regional Development of the Czech Republic were created, the Convention on Public Administration Reform was adopted;

5. 2000 – the Laws of the Czech Republic "On Regions" and "On Elections to Local Self-Government Bodies" were adopted, and 14 regions were defined as the highest territorial units of local self-government. Since 2001, the stage of consolidation of democracy has begun in the Czech Republic. The consolidation of democracy and the European integration of the Czech Republic became the defining processes for decentralization and rethinking the role of the local self-government institution. Since 1990, these processes have been synchronized with the construction of the self-governing model, its consolidation in the Constitutional Law (1997) and the Law "On Regions" (2000).

Like Slovakia, the Czech Republic also successfully implemented budget decentralization. Locally, there is an opportunity to receive income from taxes, from economic activity, from capital, to implement income grants, etc. Given the success of the territories in maintaining their own financial capacity, the influence of the central government is focused on monitoring the legality of the activities of self-governing units.

Despite the successes of decentralization and optimization of local management functions in the Czech Republic, work on the law on the territorial structure of state administration was completed in 2020. According to the parliamentarians, the law should optimize and speed up the completion of the public administration reform, which began in the late 1990s. Districts whose nominal status and authority needed resolution did not find it in the document. Instead, the law defined the rules for establishing administrative boundaries, which make it impossible for the boundaries of smaller units to go beyond the boundaries of larger units; the structure of state administration, which will consist "from below", that is, from the level of municipalities. The key goal of the innovations is to ensure the unification of the legal regulation of the division of the state, the mutual composition of territorial units, which should collectively make the entire territorial structure of state administration more transparent. Regarding the structure, 13 self-governing regions are transformed into administrative districts of municipalities with extended powers.[42]

Let's pay attention to the content of the Concept of Customer-Oriented Public Administration – 2030, which was adopted in the Czech Republic in 2020. The document envisages "strengthening the pro-client orientation of public administration in order to increase the prosperity of the Czech Republic and improve the quality of life of its citizens. Achieving the vision is conditioned by the fulfillment of a total of five strategic goals, focused on improving the quality and accessibility of public administration services, improving the functioning of the public administration system and individual institutions, increasing the competence of citizens and

---

42 Zákon č. 51/2020 Sb., o územně správním členění státu. Ministerstvo vnitra České republiky. 2021. URL: https://storymaps.arcgis.com/stories/27ada7f9e22d4e9290f1aaa5ccb31c96

the quality of their information".[43] We see in the specified Concept a strengthening of the value component of the implementation of self-governing functions in the state when the provision of administrative services from an ordinary function turns into a means of socialization, civic education and deepening the competence of the managerial elite.

The case of Czech decentralization demonstrates an effective approach to positioning both the reform and the need to transform the system of local self-government. It is about forming the image of local authorities as centers for improving the welfare of the population, increasing the comfort of the regions, and thus guaranteeing future development for the next generations. The quality of life and local services should motivate citizens to support local initiatives and directly participate in their implementation. This is the aspect of interaction in communities that does not lose its relevance for Ukraine and is the key to strengthening the comprehensive capacity of communities.

Local self-governments in Hungary acquired constitutional subjectivity later than in the other three countries of the Visegrad Group. The Constitution and the corresponding law were adopted only in 2011–2012. The progressive nature of the Constitution was that it integrated external positive experience in the organization of socio-political life and the economic sphere, but the shortcomings affected the system of local self-government.[44]

A procedural aspect that is common to all countries of the Visegrad Group is the possibility of holding local referendums. In Hungary, it is enshrined in the Law "On the Initiation of Referendums, the European Citizens' Initiative and the Procedure for Conducting Referendums" (2013).[45] There are more and more

---

43 Koncepce Klientsky orientovaná veřejná správa 2030. Ministerstvo vnitra České republiky. 2020. URL: https://www.mvcr.cz/clanek/koncepce-klientsky-orientovana-verejna-sprava-2030.aspx

44 Opinion on the new Constitution of Hungary. *Adopted by the Venice Commission at its 87th Plenary Session* (Venice, 17–18 June 2011). Venice Commission, 2011. URL: https://www.venice.coe.int/webforms/documents/default.aspx?pdffile=CDL-AD(2011)016-e

45 Törvény a népszavazás kezdeményezéséről, az európai polgári kezdeményezésről, valamint a népszavazási eljárásról (évi CCXXXVIII). Wolters Kluwer. 2013. URL: https://mkogy.jogtar.hu/jogszabaly?docid=a1300238.TV

precedents of holding such referendums in the state (2018 – 1, 2017 – 3, 2013 – 11, 2000 – 20[46]). Legislation provides for the initiation of referendums both "from above" – through the decision of the local self-government, and from below – on the initiative of local residents. Issues that can be included in the agenda of the local referendum concern local budgets and reporting on them, taxes, organizational aspects within the powers of local self-government bodies and announcement of the dissolution of a representative body. The main feature of local competences is their locality – it is possible to influence only local issues and provide only services of local importance.

With the goal of stabilizing local self-government, the Hungarian authorities have determined that the way to achieve this goal is to strengthen government control. All characteristics of the financial and property capacity of Hungarian municipalities are reduced to ascertaining the signs of budgetary centralization and state control over the exercise of financial powers in the localities. For example, the possibility of taking credit responsibility to the local level of representative power is allowed only through the appropriate procedure of agreement with the center. Therefore, the formation of local self-government in Hungary is considered an ongoing process, often referring not to the concept of decentralization but pointing to the likelihood of recentralization. The risks associated with the conventionality or artificiality of the implemented decentralization, before the completion of the entire complex of system transformations, are also relevant for Ukraine. The example of Hungary shows the consequences of a lack of internal motivation and external control. In our opinion, the Swedish version of the organization of supervision over the implementation of management powers could prevent the negative consequences of such defects.

The common past and aspirations for the further development of national statehoods have determined a significant similarity in the modeling of local self-government in the Baltic countries. Latvia, Lithuania and Estonia began to form self-governing structures

---

46 Emiatt sem kell szégyenkeznie Magyarországnak. *Rigo Kiadója A Mediaworks Hungary*. 2018. URL: https://www.origo.hu/itthon/20180123-nepszavazasok-es-helyi-referendumok-magyarorszagon.html

at the beginning of the 20th century. These processes were reset
with the beginning of the Soviet occupation, and until the early
1990s, a simple one-level system of local self-government functioned in all three countries. With the restoration of statehood, the
Baltic countries implemented a decentralization course with real
empowerment of territorial authorities. There was a transition to
a two-level model of local self-government, which is currently pre-
served only in Latvia and is in the process of reform.

If Lithuania and Estonia institutionalized local self-government
through the constitutional consolidation of its subjectivity, Latvia
uses the Law "On Municipalities" (1994). The Law describes in detail the competences of local self-government bodies and most of
the clauses of the European Charter of Local Self-Government
(which was ratified by the parliament in 1996). We would like to
note that the Latvian Constitution establishes the right of citizens
to "participate in the activities of the state and local self-government bodies" (Article 101).[47] In March 2022, the Seimas adopted the
Law on "Local Referendums", which strengthens the right of local
residents to influence the strategy of sustainable development of
the region, solve infrastructure issues and initiate the dissolution
of the local council.[48] Referendums are initiated, financed and held
locally with the possibility of obtaining methodological assistance
from the Central Election Commission. The effectiveness of the
application of the procedure of such local referenda can be assessed from 2024, when the law enters into force. An innovative approach to expanding the toolkit of citizens' will expression on the
ground is demonstrated by Estonia, which introduced E-voting in
the early 2000s. However, the example of Estonia is almost unique
both against the background of the Baltic neighbors and all the
states analyzed in the monograph. It is about the fact that almost
a third of the country's population lives in the capital – the city
of Tallinn, and in general, Estonia is characterized by the attraction of citizens to large urban centers, where jobs, quality services,

---

47 Latvijas Republikas Satversme. (Latvijas Satversmes Sapulces 1922. gada 15.
februāra kopsēdē pieņemtā). *Latvijas Republikas tiesību akti.* URL: https://likumi.
lv/ta/id/57980-latvijas-republikas-satversme
48 Vietējo pašvaldību referendumu likums (Likums stājas spēkā 2024. gada 1.
janvārī.). *Latvijas Republikas tiesību akti.* URL: https://likumi.lv/ta/id/331194-vie-
tejo-pasvaldibu-referendumu-likums

convenient logistics, etc. are concentrated. Therefore, the problem of the development of rural areas became even deeper, and the central government held the opinion that the effectiveness of the modernization of local self-government is directly related to the success of the administrative-territorial reform.

Another shortcoming is the weak financial autonomy of the regions of Estonia. About a third of local government revenue comes in the form of a grant from the central government, and the share of local tax revenue was the lowest in Europe (3.5 %). For comparison, in the above-mentioned Sweden, Finland and Denmark, this indicator was from 35 % to 55 %.[49] Therefore, the decentralization path of Estonia was completely synchronized with the reorganization of the territorial structure and went through the stages of uniting local self-government bodies, forming a new budget strategy, changing the functions of local authorities and their financing. Currently, there are 79 communities in Estonia (15 urban and 64 rural), which have increased their financial autonomy over the past five years, but they still need to expand their tax base and motivate them to develop their business environment.

The peculiarities of the organization of local self-government in Latvia are emphasized in view of the general similarity of the content of the development of the relevant structures in all three countries of the region. They synchronized the processes of transition to a market economy: European integration, democratization and decentralization, implementation of the European Charter of Local Self-Government, etc. Researcher Yu. Kobets defines the European integration of the countries of Central and Eastern Europe as an important factor of political modernization and post-communist transition, and on the other hand, calls it a factor of complicating democratic and parliamentary processes in the candidate countries due to the imposition of a large number of draft laws.[50]

---

49 Subnational Governments in OECD Countries. URL: http://www.oecd.org/regional/Subnational-governments-in-OECD-Countries-Key-Data-2018.pdf
50 Кобець Ю. Особливості регіональної політики сучасної Греції крізь призму політики Європейського Союзу. *Вісник Прикарпатського університету. Серія «Політологія».* 2016. №10. С. 113–117.

It is important that the ideology of modern European modernization of self-government is connected with two key principles –
subsidiarity and transparency. The first involves state management "from the bottom up!", that is, giving local managers such
scope of competences that allows effective and efficient solving of
social problems and requests on the ground. The second strengthens "the expansion of public participation in the processes of defining the goals and programs of social development, developing
plans and making decisions within the framework of state programs and projects, as well as their implementation".[51] In fact,
these two principles enable the institutional viability of such characteristics of state policy as local (subsidiary) and self-governing
(transparent).

All these principles are the basis of the decentralization reform
in Ukraine, and some of them have even been implemented, for example, in modern centers for the provision of administrative services by local self-government bodies, in the functioning of online
tools for communication with the population (electronic reception
rooms, offices, etc.).

Another common feature for the cases studied in the subsec-
tion is the practice of consolidation/unification of self-governing
units with a simultaneous increase in their real powers, the fundamental ones of which receive a constitutional definition. And if
during the period of democratic transformations of local self-government models in the EU countries, the issues of legal personality
of local representative authorities, procedures for their formation
and powers in the field of education, health care, local infrastructure projects, etc. were the priorities. Subsequently, the focus of
the reforms focused on ensuring property rights for communities,
budgetary decentralization and self-sufficiency mechanisms of local self-government (through taxes, grants, subsidies, etc.). We will
also emphasize the importance of various associations and unions
of local self-governments (Denmark, Finland, Lithuania, Sweden,
Latvia, Estonia, etc.), whose main task is the representation of interests in relations with government structures.

---

51 Оржель О., Палій. О. Європейський досвід державного управління: курс лекцій.
Київ: Вид-во НАДУ, 2007. 76 с.

However, the rules and principles by which the multi-level power structure is constructed in various European countries cannot be considered universal, and their relatively successful experience is not suitable for full imitation. This is primarily related to the nature of changes in the state, which includes historical experience, development of regions and population welfare, geographical and climatic specifics, consolidation of society and elite, mental characteristics of ethnic groups that inhabit the territories, etc.

The analyzed examples of the system of local self-government indicate that the corresponding reforms were part of global systemic transformations in the states, and their context is completely subordinated to the course of democratization of the country. With the exception of Hungary, where decentralization has declarative manifestations, the studied European practices prove that the decentralization of power corresponds to the general political trends in Europe at the same time. It also meets the consolidated request of societies for the openness and publicity of the government with the simultaneous involvement of citizens in its implementation and the development of the necessary mechanisms of public participation, primarily at the local level. For Ukraine, in the active phase of the decentralization reform, it is important to pay attention to the positive experience of reforms in countries that are territorially commensurate with it (therefore, a more in-depth analysis touched on France, Sweden, Germany) and those that have a deep-rooted historical commonality of state-building processes and implementation of the course of European integration (these are primarily the countries of the Visegrad Group).

Conceptually summarizing the logic of changing the nature of the territorial organization of power and the institutional environment of the functioning of local self-government, we highlight four of its components: awareness of the need to make changes; development of an appropriate algorithm (e.g., in the form of system reforms); implementation of the algorithm; and monitoring of current and final results.

PART 3

**Regional Analysis of the Main Trends
of Decentralization Processes
in Ukraine during Martial Law**

Decentralization in Ukraine has acquired both a legally defined content and specific directions within the horizontal division of powers between the center, region, district, city, united communities, etc. The principle of decentralization partially or fully affects all aspects of regional politics, producing challenges for local elites, civil servants, management personnel of all industries, because they all have to work under new scope of powers and with a different level of responsibility. Mastering such experience takes place in real time. On the one hand, this makes it possible to quickly identify all the shortcomings and miscalculations of the reform; on the other hand, due to the identified contradictions, it slows down the process of approving new opportunities for local communities.

Decentralization in the systemic dimension does not mean moving away from the center, because the center in a unitary state remains a monopoly in making important political decisions. Instead, it is about transferring part of the powers that primarily concern local affairs to other – regional levels. They are represented by local self-governments, territorial communities, councils of various levels, their heads, executive committees, headmen of local self-government units and bodies of self-organization of the population. All of them were already formed under the new legislation based on the principle of decentralization. Understanding that decentralization is not a one-time process with immediate and clearly predictable consequences, one can casually emphasize the phenomenon of destatization of political governance. It is researched by political scientist N. Vinnikova. In her opinion, the destatization of political governance, which occurs due to the splitting of national powers between networks of state, transnational, private and public entities, changes the structural modality of the processes of legitimization of political decisions from binary – "citizens-government" to multiple – multi-actor[52]. We believe that in the conditions of decentralization, such authorized actors become, in particular, communities and their residents. The researcher argues the importance of one of the derivatives of such multi-actorness: increasing political legitimacy, which is achieved through a high level of democracy at the entrance, public governance, informal supervision and control, advocacy and awareness

---

52 Вінникова Н. Проблема легітимації політичних рішень у контексті деетатизації політичного урядування. Політикус. 2019. № 1. С. 29.

raising. These features are inherent in the direct course of decentralization in the local areas.

Specialists of the National Institute of Strategic Studies distinguish two stages of the decentralization reform, which, together with the reform of the territorial organization of power, aims to "ensure the proper capacity of territorial communities, first of all, to provide public services"[53]. Consequently:

–   the first stage is devoted to the establishment of the key normative legal framework regarding the capacity of communities. First of all, it was about the definition of "capable community". Therefore, the gaps in the Law of Ukraine "On Voluntary Unification of Territorial Communities" were filled with the Methodology of Formation of Capable Territorial Communities. The final formulation of capable territorial communities took place in 2020, by which they are interpreted as "territorial communities of villages (villages, towns), which, as a result of voluntary association, are able to independently or through relevant local self-governments ensure the appropriate level of service provision, in particular in the field of education, culture, health care, social protection, housing and communal services, taking into account human resources, financial support and infrastructure development of the corresponding administrative-territorial unit". It is significant that in the issue of the capacity of communities, a leading vector – financial – appeared, because the calculation of the financial capacity of the UTc (united territorial communities) provided an opportunity to further develop a local development strategy. At the same time, the fragmentedness of this approach was criticized, based on the need for institutional and approbation inclusion in the agenda of institutional, regulatory, legal and resource aspects of the capacity of the UTc;

–   the beginning of the second stage of the decentralization reform is dated to 2019. The need to increase the capacity of UTc was emphasized, first of all, regarding the provision of public services. Experts emphasize the logic of the transition from the voluntary stage to the stage of a well-founded process of formation of UTc with the use of administrative incentives. Thus, according

53 Жаліло Я. Децентралізація і формування політики регіонального розвитку в Україні.Київ: НІСД, 2020. 153 с.

to the government Plan of measures for the implementation of a new stage of reforming local self-government and territorial organization of power in Ukraine for 2019–2021, the goal was declared – to develop and make changes to the perspective plans for the formation of territories of oblast communities by May 1, 2020. The communities would fully cover the territories, taking into account the government's methodology for the formation of capable territorial communities. The process turned out to be problematic and controversial due to the fact that during the approbation it was pointed out that the interests of all parties were not taken into account during the preparation of the specified documents. Despite all the nuances of decentralization processes, local elections were held in Ukraine that met the norms of the new electoral legislation (Electoral Code, 2019).[54]

In the monograph, we focus on the characteristics of the current, third stage and identify trends. Our task is to avoid re-analysis of those aspects that have already been repeatedly studied by scientists and experts during 2014–2019 to identify those aspects of decentralization processes in the regions that will allow us to expand our understanding of the course of fundamental systemic reform in the state. First of all, let's try to characterize the communities' capacity in more depth, and not only the financial capacity.

Analyzing the level of actual, rather than formal capacity of territorial communities, experts highlight the following urgent tasks for the state:

- to minimize the risks of recognition by the Cabinet of Ministers of Ukraine of new UTc (united territorial communities) as capable purely in view of the need to accelerate the pace of formation of united territorial communities;
- to assess the actual capacity of those formed TSOs that do not fulfill their extended powers to provide basic public services at the appropriate level.[55]

If the question of determining the capacity or inability of territorial communities was on the agenda of decentralization, then in

---

54 Жаліло Я. Децентралізація і формування політики регіонального розвитку в Україні.Київ: НІСД, 2020. 153 с. -С.8–11.
55 Жаліло Я. Децентралізація і формування політики регіонального розвитку в Україні.Київ: НІСД, 2020. 153 с. – С.11.

2021–2022 these aspects were already regulated. There were only isolated cases of appeals by local councils regarding the probable insolvency of certain communities. For example, such a situation occurred in April 2021 in the Poltava region, where the Prylutsk district council turned to the regional state administration with a proposal to recognize the Ladan community as insolvent. The reason is supposed to be financial failure, which was argued by the refusal of the village council to finance the local medical facility.[56] In fact, the issue of communal property and its maintenance is still an unsettled part of the decentralization process.

Factors that contributed to the formation of regional political processes and that were highlighted by Professor A. Romaniuk:

- the departure from the authoritarian structure of Soviet society and post-Soviet Ukraine with the simultaneous gradual spread of the principles of democracy and the activities of democratic institutions gradually lead to the spread of democratic practices;
- expansion of powers of regional structures, increase of funding sources/revenues for local budgets;
- the local elections of 2020, which, along with the fierce struggle between political actors for entry into representative and executive institutions at the regional, local and united territorial communities level, revealed the emergence of new powerful political actors at the regional level – regional and local political parties.[57]

As the researcher P. Sayenko notes, the development strategy of the united territorial community should be characterized by several essential features:

- focuses on those areas of community development that represent the greatest chance for it in the future;
- is characterized by a precise, logical approach that follows from the strategic directions of development in the system: strategic goals, operational goals and tasks for implementation;

---

56 Конфлікт Прилуцької райради та Ладанської громади. *Громади Чернігівщини.* 2021. URL: https://otg.cn.ua/2021/04/02/news-gromady/ladanska/konflikt-prylutskoyi-rajrady-ta-ladanskoyi-gromady/

57 Романюк А. Методологічні основи виборчих досліджень. Теоретичні та практичні аспекти проведення виборчих кампаній. *Сучасні методи та інструменти політичної науки: колективна монографія.* Львів: Львівський національний університет імені Івана Франка, 2020. С. 182–212

- outlines the competitive advantages of the community in relation to the immediate and distant environment – creates a strategy for dynamic development;
- is the result of the work of representatives of all groups of the community, starting with the local government, organization and institutions of the council and ending with residents. This allows you to receive proposals for goals and objectives from all interested parties, as well as the perception of local community representatives of decisions and tasks that are adopted within the framework of the strategy;
- related to other strategic documents.[58]

Analyzed documents[59,60,61,62] – and among them – strategies for the development and sustainable development of communities, development plans and strategic development plans cover the activities of urban, village and rural united territorial communities. Among the primary conclusions, we note the following:
- firstly, the structurally considered plans and strategies are quite similar, they contain monitoring of the socio-economic

58 Савчин М. (у співавт.). *Упровадження децентралізації публічної влади в Україні: національний і міжнародний аспекти.* Ужгород: TIMPANI, 2015. 216 с.

59 Стратегічний план розвитку Кам'янської міської об'єднаної територіальної громади на період 2019–2028 рр. *Кам'янська міська рада:* Офіційний вебсайт. URL: https:// kammiskrada.gov.ua/wp-.pdf; Стратегія розвитку Бахмутської міської ОТГ на період до 2027 р. *Офіційний сайт Бахмутської міської ради.* 2022. URL: https://drive.google. com.;Стратегія розвитку Березнегуватської селищної ради на період до 2027 р. *Березнегуватська громада:* Офіційний вебсайт. URL: https://berezneguvatska-gromada.gov. ua;Стратегія розвитку Вчорайшенської сільської об'єднаної територіальної громади до 2027 р. *Вчорайшенська громада:* Офіційний вебсайт. URL: https://vchorayshenska-gromada.gov.ua/docs/461791/; Стратегія розвитку Гребінківської міської об'єднаної територіальної громади до 2028 р. Гребінківська міська об'єднана територіальна громада: *Офіційний вебсайт.* 2022. URL: http://www.hrebinka.org.ua/data/files/new/ strategiya/strateg_final2.pdf

60 Населення України. *Державна служба статистики:* Офіційний вебресурс. URL: https://ukrstat.gov.ua/operativ/operativ2007/ds/nas_rik/nas_u/nas_rik_u.html

61 План реалізації Стратегії розвитку Білокуракинської об'єднаної територіальної громади 2020–2022 рр. *Білокуракинська громада:* Офіційний вебсайт. 2022. URL: https://bilokurakynska-gromada.gov.ua/strategichnij-plan-stalogo-rozvytku-bilo-kurakinskoi-selischnoi-teritorialnoi-gromadi-do-2026-roku-13-54-37-09-12-2016/

62 Регіональна програма розвитку міжнародного співробітництва Чернівецької області на 2021–2023 роки. *Чернівецька обласна державна адміністрація:* Офіційний вебсайт. URL: https://bukoda.gov.ua/storage/app/sites/23/Prohramy/dep%20comm/ rehionalna-prohrama-rozvytku-mizhnarodnoho-spivrobitnytstva-chernivetskoyi-oblasti-na-2021-2023-roky.pdf

state of the community, SWOT and sometimes PEST analysis of the environment, vision of the development of UTC, plans (detailed with and without defined future indicators), sectoral approach regarding goals and priorities, financial component, monitoring mechanism;

- secondly, developers often use the help of international and Ukrainian profile programs, which are designed to systematize and deepen the experience of united communities in Ukraine regarding strategic planning. Among them are the USAID programs "Decentralization brings better results and efficiency" (DOBRE) and "PULSE", the "U-LEAD with Europe" project, the Swiss-Ukrainian DECIDE project, etc.;

- thirdly, the term of implementation of the developed plans does not exceed 12 years (12 years is included in only one of the analyzed strategies), and on average it is 7 years.

Therefore, both the community development plans, which became the subject of the monograph, and a significant part of the accompanying documents studied cover time frames that are not tied to the term of office of one or another council, that is, they are not measured by a conditional "distance" between 2020 (the previous local elections) and 2025 (next local elections). On the contrary, the work of councils of various convocations is oriented to the inter-election period. We will immediately emphasize that the period 2021–2027 is connected with the action of the "State Regional Development Strategy for 2021–2027", the "National Economic Strategy for the Period Until 2030" and the already mentioned international projects designed to help the UTC organize planning own work development. However, we consider the strengthening of institutional memory as an important state-building element to be a more important aspect. We agree with Professor G. Shchedrova's definition of institutional memory, which she defines as the ability of the governance system to store accumulated information about past political practices, including the assessment of actions, decisions and their consequences, which in the form of experience finds continuation in the analysis or implementation of policy.[63] The political scientist connects the provision of insti-

63 Щедрова Г. Інституційна пам'ять: концептуалізація в політологічному дискурсі. Політикус. 2021. № 5. С. 17–22.

tutional memory with people (officials) who actually implement certain programs and reforms within the limits of their powers. Therefore, we claim that the lack of synchronization of strategic development planning of united territorial communities with election cycles supports not only economic management practices but also the further implementation of the decentralization reform.

United communities in Ukraine are forming their own vision of development and determining priorities. At the same UTCs must maneuver between the norms established by legislation, clearly understand the limits of their authority, not duplicate, but complement the previously developed regional development strategies of each region. Indeed, the structure of the mentioned strategies is adaptive to the needs of the UTC, and the regional development strategies were agreed with the State Strategy of Regional Development for 2021–2027; however, the resource base and own potential of the communities differ significantly from the regional ones.[64] Therefore, the emphasis, it would seem, on the details (such as specific addresses where there is a need to arrange residential areas, the exact names of institutions, sections of roads, locations of emergency trees, a list of specialists in demand in specific settlements) are important for planning and calculating one's own forces and format a team that should be responsible for different areas of work.

We consider the fact of developing programs for the development of local self-government organizations to be evidence of a responsible attitude towards the implementation of new functions by the new system of local self-government. The development of regional development strategies is the authority, not the duty, of village, settlement, city and district councils in state regional policy. The key priority for the development of communities (as well as more globally – regions) is the economy – its growth, optimization and reorientation to internal resources, as evidenced by the approved directions of state regional policy. This includes stimulation and support of local initiatives for the effective use of the

---

64 Постанова Кабінету міністрів України «Про затвердження Державної стратегії регіонального розвитку на 2021–2027 роки» від 5.08.2020 р. Верховна Рада України: Офіційний вебпортал. URL: https://zakon.rada.gov.ua/laws/show/695-2020-%D0%BF#Text

internal potential of regions to create and maintain a full-fledged living environment, improving the quality of life of people; reduction of territorial differentiation according to indicators of socio-economic development; formation of competitiveness of regions; formation of a united state in social, humanitarian, economic, ecological, security and spatial dimensions; adaptation of the regional economy and human habitat to climate changes, strengthening the resilience of territorial communities to climatic, demographic and economic challenges; improvement of material, financial, informational, personnel and other resource support for the development of regions, assistance in the exercise of powers by local self-government bodies, etc.

The targeted search covered the issues of how local communities are included in the implementation of international cooperation and the promotion of the European integration course, which are defined in different formulations by the norms of the current legislation and the functions of local self-government bodies. Here we will single out certain trends that have a logical explanation:

–   directions of international cooperation and their content depend on the previous experience of communities participating in relevant projects and programs (U-LEAD with Europe, the International Renaissance Fund, eTwinning, Erasmus+, the United States Agency for International Development (USAID), the European Bank for Reconstruction and Development, Partnership for the development of cities – PROMIS, etc.). Such experience leads to detailed strategies for attracting international donor aid in the social sphere, infrastructure, creating additional educational conditions for young people, restoration projects, etc. Lack of experience is the reason for the emphasis on informing communities about international projects and programs, identifying participation in them as an important perspective (primarily in terms of attracting investments, grants, donor support). By default, the documents indicate the continuation of the experience of participation of local industry entities in international projects, exhibitions, forums, international certification at productions, etc.;

–   the geography of communities determines the priority of cross-border international cooperation, which, as a rule, is already based on constructive cooperation with foreign neighbors. At the current stage of the development of Ukraine's international relations with foreign institutions, good-neighborliness is moving from the informational and educational sphere to the realm of systemic infrastructure projects for the construction of roads, checkpoints, financing of construction and major repairs of educational, cultural, health care institutions, etc. The usual practice of recent years is the development of target regional programs of international cooperation in the regions (for 2021–2023, they were adopted in Chernivtsi region, for 2022–2026 – in Ivano-Frankivsk region, for 2022–2024 – in Rivne region, for 2021 -2025 – in Dnipropetrovsk, etc.).[65; 66; 67]

- the European integration context of forming visions of regional development of communities is quite blurred, as in the wording that "the inclusion of local self-government in European integration processes is a guarantee of increasing the investment attractiveness of regions".[68] The approach of orienting local development planning to the seven-year cycles of planning and budgetary funding of the European Union looks more constructive.[69]

- finally, we note that the strategies for the development of territorial communities are mainly open to information because their public discussion in the approbation conditions of the de-

65 Населення України. *Державна служба статистики*: Офіційний вебресурс. URL: https://ukrstat.gov.ua/operativ/operativ2007/ds/nas_rik/nas_u/nas_rik_u.html

66 Регіональна програма розвитку міжнародного співробітництва Чернівецької області на 2021–2023 роки. *Чернівецька обласна державна адміністрація*: Офіційний вебсайт. URL: https://bukoda.gov.ua/storage/app/sites/23/Prohramy/dep%20comm/rehionalna-prohrama-rozvytku-mizhnarodnoho-spivrobitnytstva-chernivetskoyi-oblasti-na-2021-2023-roky.pdf

67 Про схвалення проекту регіональної цільової програми розвитку міжнародного співробітництва та промоції Івано-Франківської області на 2022–2026 роки: *Розпорядження ОДА*. Офіційний вебсайт Івано-Франківської обласної державної адміністрації. URL: https://www.if.gov.ua/npas/pro-shvalennya-proektu-regionalnoyi-cilovoyi-programi-rozvitku-mizhnarodnogo-spivrobitnictva-ta-promociyi-ivano-frankivskoyi-oblasti-na-2022-2026-roki

68 Стратегія розвитку Преображенської сільської об'єднаної територіальної громади на 2021–2027 рр. *Преображенська об'єднана територіальна громада*: Офіційний вебсайт. URL: https://preobrazhenska-gromada.gov.ua/plan-zahodiv-na-20212023-roki- /

69 Проєкт Стратегії сталого розвитку Нетішинської міської об'єднаної територіальної громади на період до 2028 р. *Нетішинська міська рада*: Офіційний вебсайт. URL: https://www.netishynrada.gov.ua/DOC/publ- x

centralization context of state formation is extremely important. As of 2023, the vast majority of territorial communities have functional and updated websites, administer their own pages in social networks, and pay attention to the interactivity of their public activities.

We will separately consider the functioning of the institution of local self-government in the conditions of martial law. These circumstances, after the full-scale military invasion of the Russian Federation, affected all spheres of socio-political, economic and cultural life. In May 2022, the Law "On Amendments to Certain Laws of Ukraine Regarding the Functioning of the Civil Service and Local Self-Government During Martial Law" was adopted. The document states that "military administrations of settlements are formed within the territories of territorial communities in which village, settlement, city councils and/or their executive bodies, and/or village, settlement, city mayors do not exercise the powers assigned to them by the Constitution and laws of Ukraine, as well as in other cases provided for by this Law. The military administration of a settlement (settlements) is headed by a chief who is appointed and dismissed by the President of Ukraine on the proposal of the General Staff of the Armed Forces of Ukraine or the relevant regional state administration. The head of the military administration of the settlement (settlements) may be appointed the relevant village, township, or city head".[70]

But the most important thing is that the Law describes changes in the limits of the authority of local communities, namely:
-   under the condition of the establishment of a military administration of a settlement, the powers of the settlement/village/city councils, its executive bodies are taken over by the military administration, and the powers of the head are taken over by the head of the military administration;
-   increasing the powers of the village, township and city head of a territorial community (where hostilities are not taking place and a military administration has not been formed), who will

70 Закон України «Про внесення змін до деяких законів України щодо функціонування державної служби та місцевого самоврядування у період дії воєнного стану» від 12.05.2022 р. *Верховна Рада України*: Офіційний вебпортал. URL: https://zakon.rada.gov.ua/laws/show/2259-IX#Text

be able to make a number of decisions on budget, personnel issues, etc. on his own;
- the head of a village, settlement, or city or the head of an executive body can individually appoint persons to positions in local self-government bodies, as well as managers of communal enterprises, institutions and organizations in the sphere of management of their local self-government;
- the powers of regional (in case of occupation or encirclement of the administrative center of the region) and district councils are taken over by the regional/district military administration.[71]

Did the local self-governments receive any benefits as a result of the adoption of the new Law? Rather, it is about the exclusive functions of village, settlement and city heads of territorial communities, on whose territory no military operations are conducted and no decision has been made to form military administrations to implement the measures of the legal regime of martial law.

The new Law defines the period of exercise of powers by military administrations, which is the period of martial law and 30 days after its termination or cancellation. The President of Ukraine, the Verkhovna Rada of Ukraine and the Cabinet of Ministers of Ukraine can influence the duration of the tenure of the head of the military administration. We will point out right away that this is not the first experience of the operation of military and military-civilian administrations with special powers in Ukraine similar authorities have been operating in the Donetsk and Luhansk regions since 2015.

The Russian-Ukrainian war, as well as the consequences caused by it, cannot be considered a trend, but in the context of the analysis of decentralization processes, we must take into account a certain pause in the full implementation of their legally established powers by communities. Another aspect is the new responsibility of communities: for individual decision-making by heads, for the accommodation of refugees, legalization of relocated businesses and enterprises, as well as open questions regarding the distribution of responsibilities and resources between elected bodies of local self-government and local executive bodies, the status and responsibil-

---

71 Падалко В. Централізація та децентралізація в організації служби в органах місцевого самоврядування: муніципально-правовий аспект. *Держава і право*. 2012. № 57. С. 123–129.

ity of local elected representatives. The positive side of the indicated state of affairs is the understanding of new challenges, the analysis of their consequences at the beginning of the war and, as a result, the inclusion of local self-government issues in the Recovery Plan developed by the National Council for the Recovery of Ukraine from the Consequences of the War.[72] Among the goals of the Plan, experts note: renewal of the administrative and territorial system; consolidation of the distribution of powers between local self-governments at all levels, as well as with local executive bodies; introduction of an effective and flexible system of training and promotion of employees of local self-governments and thus the formation of attractive and favorable working conditions in the public service; improvement of the electoral system of local elections.

To sum up, the new trends in the functioning of local self-government chronologically consist of:

- approvals of legislation – norms begin to work, and the powers defined by laws are gradually synchronized with the relevant competences of local authorities and politicians;
- assessment of the real ability of communities to independently implement initiatives of local importance, take responsibility for long-term projects, overcome contradictions regarding the delimitation of functions of local self-governments of different levels, maintenance of communal property, etc.;
- practices of strategic planning of socio-economic development of territorial communities. The planning period leads to the strengthening of institutional memory since it is not tied to electoral cycles. In the conditions of dynamic approval of their own capacity, the communities do not detail the resources, thanks to which they plan to achieve the results of industry development set in the plans. There is a certain distancing from financial assistance from the center. Synchronization of strategic development plans of communities and regions is maintained;
- the functioning of the local self-government system in the conditions of martial law, when part of the management functions is temporarily transferred to the military and military-civilian administrations.

---

72 Дацишин М. Як відновити місцеве самоврядування від наслідків війни? Українська правда. 2022. URL: https://www.pravda.com.ua/columns/2022/08/5/7362004/

PART 4

Implementation of the Electoral Mechanism for the Formation of Representative Democracy in United Territorial Communities

The local elections in Ukraine, which took place in the fall of 2020, were not perceived as an important political process in the country. The participants in the election race competed for real power, primarily financial, which the representative bodies of local self-government received as a result of the successful launch of the decentralization reform and changes in the principles of local self-government. Let's emphasize that these were actually the first elections to the united territorial communities. Another feature of the election process was the active participation of political parties, sometimes party projects, which were created specifically for these elections. It should be noted that according to the voting results, more than 80 % of the elected local deputies were nominated by local organizations of political parties.[73]

Since 2014, decentralization has been ongoing in Ukraine, which the current governments presented as one of the few successful reforms. Part of the reform of local self-government and administrative-territorial system consists in the transfer from the "center" to the "localities" of a significant part of powers, resources and responsibility. The concept of the reform of local self-government and territorial organization of power assumed voluntariness, and before the next local elections in 2020, the communities had to unite and go to the elections in new associations.[74]

Despite the statement about possible early local elections, the representatives of the monomajority in the parliament voiced the main theses regarding the local elections of 2020: local elections were to be held within the terms stipulated by the Constitution of Ukraine; it was proposed to make changes to the Electoral Code designed to eliminate technical inconsistencies in the rules regarding the preparation and conduct of elections; additional barriers for the participation of parties in local elections will not be introduced; electoral legislation should preserve the right of a person to self-nominate for the post of mayor (village, settlement,

73 *Центральна виборча комісія:* Офіційний вебсайт. URL: https://www.cvk.gov.ua/vibory_category/mistsevi-vibori/vibori-deputativ-verhovnoi-radi-avtonom-noi-respubliki-krim-oblasnih-rayonnih-miskih-rayonnih-silskih-selishhnih-rad-25-10-2020.html#

74 Мельничук В. Місцеві вибори – 2020 в умовах децентралізації влади: виклики для місцевого самоврядування. *Вісник Прикарпатського університету. Серія «Політологія».* 2020. № 14. С. 59–64.

city mayor), and the realization of such a right should not depend on party membership; the cash deposit in local elections should be reduced and the current 90,000 voter barrier in cities, which involves the introduction of a proportional election system, should be reduced as well.

Local elections were held under the new Electoral Code, which entered into force on January 1, 2020. It was not the first time that changes in electoral legislation were primarily of interest to local self-government representatives. Book four of the Electoral Code is dedicated to local elections, which are now based on the following principles:

- elections of deputies of the village, settlement and city councils in territorial communities with the number of voters up to 10,000 people are held according to the majoritarian system of relative majority in multi-mandate electoral districts into which the territory of the respective territorial community is divided. No less than two and no more than four deputies may be elected in each such district;

- elections of deputies of regional, district and city district councils, as well as deputies of city, village and settlement councils (also in UTC with a number of voters of 10,000 or more) are held according to the system of proportional representation based on open electoral lists of local organizations of political parties in territorial electoral districts, into which a single multi-mandate electoral district is divided;

- elections of the village, township and city (city with the number of voters up to 75 thousand people) mayor are held according to the majoritarian electoral system of the relative majority in a single single-mandate village, township and city electoral district, which coincides with the territory of the village, township and city according to the administrative-territorial organization or the territory of a village, settlement and urban territorial community;

- elections of the mayor of a city (a city with a number of voters of 75 thousand or more) are held according to the majoritarian electoral system of the absolute majority in a single single-mandate city electoral district;

- the electoral system, according to which the elections of deputies of the city, village, settlement councils and the mayor are held, is determined based on the number of voters who have the right to vote in the relevant local elections, as of the first day of the month preceding the month in which the election process begins with relevant local elections.[75]

Regarding the connection between local elections and the decentralization reform, it is worth pointing out the conflict, which is that decentralization did not begin, but ended with elections. Regional state administrations prepared projects, had to conduct local consultations, draw up plans and submit them to the government for approval. Instead, the rapid approach of local elections motivated the Verkhovna Rada to change the model of adopting long-term plans, and the Cabinet of Ministers independently determined the center and borders of the community. It was a kind of completion of the decentralization process in manual mode, a process in which several relevant ministers made corrections.

It is worth emphasizing the value of those elections. During the seven waves of creation of communities, the focus of the elections was in the first place. Both political parties, community leaders and the President's Administration focused on the political component, and the community structure was formed depending on who would win the first election. After receiving maps of the regions, the American principle of gerrymandering was applied, that is, the formation of electoral districts to suit certain political forces. It obviously contradicted both the reform and the normal functioning of local self-government, because communities were formed for certain groups of voters. And if a party or a financial and industrial group predicted that it would not be able to gain power in a big city, it created a community around the city. To combat such phenomena, the Concept was not enough, because its institutional influence was definitely inferior to a full-fledged law. It became the Electoral Code, which included the changes regarding local elections described above.

According to the Election Code and the Constitution of Ukraine, regular local elections are held on the last Sunday of October of the fifth year of the mandate of the councils, heads of councils elected at the previous regular local elections. The only conditions for the

---

75 Виборчий кодекс України від 19.12.2019 р. *Верховна Рада України: Офіційний веб-портал*. URL: https://zakon.rada.gov.ua/laws/show/396-20#Text

postponement of regular local elections may be: the introduction of martial law/state of emergency or the introduction of amendments to the Constitution to determine a different term of office of the subjects. However, in 2020, the elections were influenced by another factor not provided for by regulatory documents – the statistics of the incidence of the coronavirus. In a number of countries around the world, against the background of the pandemic, they decided to postpone elections of various scales – presidential (Poland, Moldova, Iceland), parliamentary (Montenegro, Lithuania, Georgia, Romania, Croatia) and local (Spain, Austria, Great Britain, France). But these countries mostly postponed elections that had to take place in the near future, while the Ukrainian elections were still six months away.

When it is said that fundamental reforms in Ukraine are carried out under permanent force majeure circumstances, it is worth pointing out that their course also differs from established standards. For example, international standards of the European Union forbid changing the territorial organization of elections, the electoral system and the way election commissions are formed less than a year before the start of the campaign. Instead, in the process of preparing for the 2020 local elections in Ukraine, the following changes took place:

- territorial organization of elections – the parliament has not yet voted for the resolution on the liquidation of old and the creation of new, consolidated districts ("rayons"), so the Central Election Commission could not undertake the full preparation of the election campaign;
- the electoral system – amendments to the Electoral Code, which were planned to be put to the vote, plunged even the smallest villages with 10 thousand voters into political chaos and confrontation;
- the method of formation of election commissions with the prerogative of parliamentary groups.[76]

Such elections – on a new administrative-territorial basis, with a new Electoral Code and a new electoral system – have not yet

---

76 Мельничук В. Місцеві вибори – 2020 в умовах децентралізації влади: виклики для місцевого самоврядування. *Вісник Прикарпатського університету. Серія «Політологія»*. 2020. № 14. С. 59–64.

been held in Ukraine. But the elections were held with a lower turnout (the first round – 37 %, the second – 29 %) than during the local elections of 2015 (the first round – 47 %, the second – 34 %). We see several reasons for such indicators: firstly, people in general are tired of politics, having experienced difficult presidential and parliamentary elections; secondly, it is worth considering the factor of the coronavirus pandemic and the restrictions caused by it; thirdly, low turnout in local elections is a general world trend (it is not for nothing that the stereotype of "second-order elections" has developed). Another assumption expressed by expert circles concerns voters' misunderstanding of the current Electoral Code, which may have reduced their interest in participating in the electoral process.

The trends resulting from the elections, on the one hand, were predictable; on the other hand, it could be considered a certain signal for the authorities regarding the possible consequences of the revenge of pro-Russian political forces, attraction to local elites, who, it would seem, discredited themselves. It is obvious that it was not possible to repeat the results of the parliamentary elections. It is believed that the parliamentary parties lost the local elections, primarily because none of them won them.

Let's also pay attention to the election technologies used by the headquarters of local organizations of political parties and analyzed by the researcher V. Komarnytskyi:

-   use of duplicate candidates, or "clones" (candidates with exactly the same name). Election campaigns in Uman, Uzhhorod, Odesa, Cherkasy and other cities were distinguished by this. It is significant that some of these candidates deliberately changed their names during the year before the elections, which is not prohibited by law. However, in some cases, the Central Election Commission canceled the registration of "clones";
-   electoral tourism – a mass change of voting place by voters. Its importance and influence is determined by the fact that in local elections the "value" of the mandate was calculated by several hundred votes. It is about the "migration" of voters within the region, as well as about nationwide tours, which, according to the experts of the "Committee of Voters of Ukraine" and the public network "OPORA", can distort the election results. Such cases were recorded in Odesa Region, Lviv Region,

Khmelnytskyi Region, Zakarpattia, Zhytomyr Region and Ternopil Region, where the number of voters increased by 100–750 people in certain communities;

- bribery of voters and "carousel" technology on election day – this practice is not new; it is legally recognized as a crime (Article 160 of the Criminal Code of Ukraine). The concepts of "net" and "carousel" have long been ingrained in the Ukrainian election lexicon, and the 2020 election campaign was marked by 191 statements to police regarding possible bribery of voters on the day of voting alone;

- the spread of fakes, i.e. the discrediting information or reports about the alleged withdrawal of competitors' candidacies from the elections;

- poll speculations, when those that were not listed on the official website by the Central Election Commission at the beginning of the campaign for technical reasons were deliberately removed from the list of political parties. It is worth noting that political parties, as participants in the 2020 local elections, did not sufficiently use the sociological toolkit to analyze the electoral field, develop and implement an election strategy, etc. Figures submitted by party members in the form of agitation or counter-agitation often did not have original data, references to sociological agencies; instead, they were argued by "closed" or "party" sociology, which was often based on a survey on the platform of social networks or local information sites or Telegram-channels. During the day, the voter could receive several rating lists, the configurations of which contradicted each other;

- manipulation of party branding – when parties deliberately choose similar brand books or "neutral" political appeals, frame themselves in party colors before voting and on "day of silence".[77]

---

[77] Комарницький В. Роль партійного чинника в реалізації електоральних стратегій (на прикладі місцевих виборів 2020 року). *Вісник Національного технічного університету України «Київський політехнічний інститут». Серія «Політологія. Соціологія. Право».* 2020. № 1 (45). С. 19–24. URL: http://visnyk-psp.kpi.ua/article/view/226468/226072

According to the conclusion of the researcher A. Romaniuk, there was an increase in the importance of the use of mass media and social networks, the involvement of lawyers, as well as a limited time for the election campaign, even when party organizations and individual candidates begin to prepare for the elections in advance and carry out various actions. They are aimed at increasing the recognition and commitment of voters, the period from the official start of the election campaign to the day of voting is characterized by hyperactivity. In these conditions, political parties that have resources and count on a positive result formally at a certain stage of their functioning experienced/are experiencing a dilemma – to make elections based on existing party members or to attract specialists and hired workers. There is always the option of combining these two components.[78]

It should be noted that parties played an important role in local elections. Even the mayors of cities whose nominations did not require party affiliation of the candidates turned out to be nominees of the parties for 80 %. Innovations of the Electoral Code were both approved and criticized at the same time, in particular, regarding the role of parties in the local election process. On the one hand, party chaos gained new momentum – party projects were created, local parties "revived", a struggle began within grassroots party cells, and pressure from the party center intensified. On the other hand, regional organizational structures of political parties began to fulfill their basic function of representing the interests of citizens, and not, as in previous years, of reinforcing key party messages and promoting the party brand on the periphery.

The described changes determine our conclusion about the deepening of democratic principles precisely because of the specifics of the 2020 local elections:
- during the struggle for voters' votes, it was impossible to avoid political communication, which shapes the political elite's perception of the needs and requests of the region and its residents;
- in 2020, the local elections did not become a rehearsal for the parliamentary and presidential elections but were supposed to

---

78 Романюк А. Особливості та тенденції трансформації членської бази в політичних партіях України. *Вісник Львівського університету. Серія «Філософсько-політологічні студії»*. 2022. № 43. С. 295–305. – С.300.

consolidate the positions of the already active players in the political field, primarily the presidential force and the parties that got into the parliament. Therefore, political actors had to continue the dialogue with the electorate, including responding to the claims of the elite who passed the 2019 selection;

- the specifics of the new legislation led to the transformation of the content and role of party branches, which ceased to be a temporary and auxiliary phenomenon, and turned into important platforms for establishing information and communication links between the center and regions, local authorities and the community;

- per citizen, there are significantly more local deputies of various levels than parliamentarians. As civil society matures, this fact can be turned into a tool for monitoring the activities of local self-government bodies. And as Professor S. Derevyanko rightly observes, awareness and compliance by the authorities and political elites of the obligation to obtain by voting consent to institutional changes or the need to "consult with the people" on important problems of national or local importance will objectively contribute to the legal provision of the establishment civil society;[79]

- we also take into account the distance between the candidate and the voter. At the local level, this distance is minimal, so it is easier to find tools for approval, consultation, control and other democratic procedures.

In a democratic society, the pluralism of social groups, the difference and diversity of their interests, and the articulation and aggregation by numerous political parties/actors of special interests in the multifaceted nature of political programs are recognized. During elections, political actors appeal to all/major groups in society or to specific groups for support. Political actors make election programs/projects the subject of communication with citizens, which provide options for social development based on the response to existing social challenges for the entire society and/or for specific social groups.

---

79 Дерев'янко С. Безпековий вимір народовладдя в умовах гібридної війни. *Держава і право.* 2020. № 87. С. 308–318.

The contradictory nature of the democratic characteristics of the 2020 local elections is attributed to the fact that the elections were competitive and complied with the electoral legislation, but such a democratic innovation as open party lists was completely discredited. In fact, we got a somewhat complicated proportional system. The candidates, trying to get to the top of their party's list, did not fully know the order of the final list, which was determined by the party's leadership apparatus. That is, we consider the approval of the transition to open lists in local elections a failure. At the same time, the elections became a litmus test for the rating of the central government, which has obviously lost its primary positions. The winners were the local oligarchic party projects, whose victory will contribute to the further atomization of the political spectrum of the state. But even such a course of events does not exclude the democratic component – all these parties were chosen by the voter in open competition. The next challenge for united communities was coalition building in councils at different levels, since it was not possible to repeat the parliamentary configuration at the local level. Local influencers did not join the central parties and did not guarantee them monopolies at the local level; instead, they registered their own political forces as all-Ukrainian parties and created a successful crash test for them. The parties "Native Transcarpathia", All-Ukrainian Association "Cherkashchany", "Block of Kernes – Successful Kharkiv!", "Party of Vinnytsia" and others became winners in their regions.

According to the final results of the local elections, the specialists of the sociological group "Rating" presented an analytical report, indicating:
- The 5 % barrier was overcome by the political parties "Servant of the People" (14.5 %), "European Solidarity" (13.7 %), "Opposition Platform – For Life" (12.5 %), "For the Future" (8 .6 %) and "Fatherland" (8.5 %). The percentages were calculated from the total number of votes of voters who supported the parties;
- the total rating of other, mostly local, parties is about 22 %;
- the combined support of the five parliamentary parties in these elections was 51 %, while in the 2019 Verkhovna Rada elections they received 78 % of the vote. At the same time, in regions where powerful local parties were not represented, parliamentary parties received significantly bigger support in local elections;

- local parties became winners in Vinnytsia ("Groysman's Ukrainian Strategy"), Zakarpattia ("Native Transcarpathia"), Poltava ("Trust"), Kharkiv ("Block of Kernes – Successful Kharkiv!"),
  Khmelnytsky ("Symchyshyn's Team"), Cherkasy ("Cherkashchany") and Chernihiv ("Native Home") regions.[80]

Finally, it is worth pointing to one more democratic procedure,
which in the context of local government is still on the waiting list.
This is an opportunity to hold local referendums, which the territorial community has the right to initiate by law.[81] However, as
already mentioned in the previous chapters, the same legislation
does not yet regulate the relevant procedure.

According to the idea of decentralization, local referendums
were supposed to become a true expression of people's power
in the community. In a more systematic manner, the procedure
would allow for the qualitative application of the principle of subsidiarity, as it would determine the priorities in solving local issues by the forces of the community, its representatives in various
councils and in communication with the central government. In
November 2012, a law was passed that defined the possibility of
holding an exclusively all-Ukrainian referendum. In the same year,
the Law "On All-Ukrainian and Local Referendums" became inval-
id; since then, we state a violation of Article 38 of the Constitution
of Ukraine, which entitles citizens to the right "to participate in
the management of state affairs, in all-Ukrainian and local referendums, to freely elect and be elected to bodies of state power and
bodies of local self-government".[82]

In May 2021, the Project of the Law on Local Referendum was registered. It also defines the tasks that the residents of the communities
will be able to solve by participating in the referendum, namely:
- approval of the charter and program of development of the
  territorial community or changes to them;

---

80 Моніторинг місцевих виборів 2020: підсумки. *Соціологічна група «Рейтинг»*.
2020.   URL: https://ratinggroup.ua/research/ukraine/monitoring_mestnyh_
vyborov_2020_itogi.html
81 Закон України «Про інвестиційну діяльність» від 18.09.1991 р. *Верховна Рада України*: Офіційний вебсайт. URL: https://zakon.rada.gov.ua/laws/show/1560-12#Text
82 Конституція України (від 28.06.1996 р. зі змінами). *Президент України*: Офіційне
інтернет-представництво. URL: https://www.president.gov.ua/ua/documents/con-
stitution/konstituciya-ukrayini-rozdil-xi

- early termination of the powers of village, settlement, city councils and their heads;
- loss of validity of the normative legal act of the local self-government or its separate provisions;
- another matter of local importance, assigned by the Constitution and laws of Ukraine to the responsibility of the territorial community, its bodies and officials.

The document is currently being reviewed by the parliamentary structures and received several dozen comments in the conclusion of the Chief Scientific and Expert Department, in particular regarding the initiators of the local referendum, the need for additional implementation of the referendum results through approval by the local self-government, establishment of the results of the will, etc. On February 10, 2022, the European Commission "For Democracy through Law" (Venice Commission) published an urgent opinion on the draft law "On Local Referendum", which contains an assessment of the compliance of the draft law with international standards. In particular, it corresponds to the updated version of the Referendum Regulations, as well as the 1990 OSCE Copenhagen Document. The commission generally positively assessed the draft law on the local referendum – both its content and the preparation process. The conclusion noted an inclusive public discussion that contributed to stakeholders' understanding of the process and increased confidence in the draft law. And the draft law itself is called "an important step on the way to holding local referendums after the repeal of the Law 'On All-Ukrainian and Local Referendums', which caused a legal vacuum in the issue of regulating the institution of local referendums".[83] At the same time, criticism by the Venice Commission and the OSCE Bureau of Democratic Institutions and Human Rights of the provisions of the draft law, which do not allow citizens of a state recognized by the Verkhovna Rada as an "aggressor state" or an "occupying state" to register as international observers during a local referendum, causes confusion. In our opinion, the level of previous intervention

---

83 Венеційська комісія оприлюднила висновок щодо законопроєкту про місцевий референдум. *Реанімаційний пакет реформ.* 2022. URL: https://rpr.org.ua/news/venetsiyska-komisiia-opryliudnyla-vysnovok-shchodo-zakonoproiektu-pro-mistsevyy-referendum/

of Russian agents in the implementation of state policy at all levels in Ukraine directly leads to catastrophic consequences for the development of the state, its security and territorial integrity, as well as for the democratic values and ideals of the entire civilized world.

Therefore, the combination of election procedures and the possibility of holding referendums at the local level will ensure the democratic principles of formation of the development directions of the UTCs and their implementation by the representative bodies of local self-government. In conditions of successfully overcoming the stages of the decentralization reform, the local level of politics can become an effective testing ground for testing democratic procedures. Equally important is the participation of the population, who will be able to directly influence the creation of the agenda for the community and set priorities in the implemented strategic development plans. Delegation under such conditions will be balanced, conscious and responsible, which at the central level still has only formal features.

The analysis of the implementation of the electoral mechanism for the formation of representative democracy at the local level, primarily on the example of the 2020 local elections, made it possible to assess the political significance of approving the new election rules. First of all, we note unprecedented attention to the campaign of political actors at the regional and central levels, which is caused, in our opinion, by the change in the scope of powers of representative authorities on the ground. The key actors here were the political parties, which for the first time encountered quality requirements for party lists and showed their unpreparedness for the updated conditions of conducting the election campaign, due to which the lists of party candidates contained a significant number of non-party participants.[84] The local elections intensified the work of the branches of political parties to improve the personnel potential or, at least, increase it. The parties, which previously acted as a kind of agents of decentralization reform, were brought to power by the existing local elites. We believe that such

---

84 Романюк А. Особливості та тенденції трансформації членської бази в політичних партіях України. *Вісник Львівського університету. Серія «Філософсько-політологічні студії»*. 2022. № 43. С. 295–305.

a result has one significant drawback – the old elites were formed in the tradition of centralized power and conditional powers of local self-government bodies, and exerted their influence behind the scenes, weakly interacting with communities. The period of time to overcome this shortcoming turned out to be too short because with the beginning of the full-scale Russian military invasion, key competences on the ground were transferred to military state administrations. Therefore, the longest election process will continue with a long trial of the entire scope of powers and legislative innovations acquired by local representative authorities.

PART 5

Institutional and Legal Features
of Cooperation between Territorial
Communities and Possibilities
of Regional International Cooperation

After the formation of united territorial communities, which included several settlements, and new zoning, the need to continue cooperation within the region did not disappear, but the process became more complicated due to the double bureaucracy. The institutional foundation of cooperation is primarily the norms of the Law of Ukraine "On Cooperation of Territorial Communities" dated June 17, 2014.[85] The law fully clarifies who, how and for what purpose can one cooperate on behalf of interested territorial communities. Moreover, self-interest and interests are the drivers of such processes: cooperation should be voluntary and mutually beneficial for the participants.

In accordance with the legislation, the subjects of cooperation are the territorial communities of villages, towns and cities, which carry it out through village, settlement and city councils in the areas of common interests of territorial communities within the powers of the relevant local self-government bodies, unless otherwise provided by law. Such cooperation is based on the principles of legality, voluntariness, mutual benefit, transparency and openness, equality of participants and mutual responsibility of cooperation subjects for its results. Forms in which communities can interact in common interests are also regulated, which is the delegation of one or more tasks with the transfer of relevant resources; the implementation of joint projects, which involves the coordination of the activities of cooperation subjects and their accumulation of resources for a specified period in order to jointly implement relevant measures; joint financing or maintenance by subjects of cooperation of enterprises, institutions and organizations of a communal form of ownership; formation by subjects of cooperation of joint communal enterprises, institutions and organizations or a joint management body for the joint performance of powers defined by law. Such cooperation is terminated in the case of prior notification by the subject of cooperation to other subjects of his cooperation with payment of compensation to them in accordance with the terms of the concluded contract.

---

85 Закон України «Про транскордонне співробітництво» від 24.06.2004 р. *Верховна Рада України*: Офіційний вебсайт. URL: https://zakon.rada.gov.ua/laws/show/1861-15#Text

During the reform of decentralization and improvement of the quality of local self-government, institutional changes should be accompanied by an improvement in the interaction of public institutions with respect to local self-governments and members of the UTC. As E. Borodin and I. Shumlyaeva point out, in Ukraine, the degree of involvement and inclusion of members of the territorial community in the process of making public-management decisions related to solving issues of local importance mainly depends on local self-government bodies. The public activity of the population is determined by the policy pursued by the local government. The authorities can convince people of the importance and necessity of the participation of residents of the territorial community in local public life and their interest in it.[86] Accordingly, cooperation with another community should be motivated by the initiative of the residents of the community, and this actualizes the procedure of public hearings and meetings as acts of direct democracy, as well as the inclusion of such activities of the UTC in their charter. Such a point of view may seem somewhat intrusive – one that does not sufficiently motivate communities to interact together. In fact, in our vision, we emphasize, firstly, the lack of experience of communities in determining the priorities of their activities, and secondly, the risks of ignoring those problems that are common to territories without reference to the borders of the UTC. As a way out of the situation, we see the joint introduction to the agenda of local government to solve issues that may concern several neighboring communities. This is where one of the formats of cooperation of territorial communities mentioned above and enshrined in the Law will come in handy.[87]

The advantages of joint implementation of initiatives for communities, according to experts, are:

- cooperation to ensure the possibility of carrying out vital functions and activities (e.g., water supply, waste disposal, operation of public transport, etc.);
- expansion of the consumer market due to inclusion of a larger

---

86 Бородін Є., Шумляєва І. Інституційно-правове забезпечення функціонування суб'єктів місцевого самоврядування в Україні. *Аспекти публічного управління*. 2021. № 3. С. 13–21.

87 Закон України «Про транскордонне співробітництво» від 24.06.2004 р. *Верховна Рада України*: Офіційний вебсайт. URL: https://zakon.rada.gov.ua/laws/show/1861-15#Text

number of consumers in receiving services, as well as reduction of production costs;
- joining efforts to attract investments;
- increasing the level of trust among creditors and the ability to attract external financing from both the state and private partners.[88]

Another aspect of the local self-government system that requires special attention is the need and opportunities for cooperation between regional (oblast) councils, which have received a significant amount of authority, and district (rayon) councils, whose territorial authority has undergone significant scaling, while the administrative authority remains undefined. The district and regional levels of the administrative-territorial system, despite being enshrined in the Concept of Reforming Local Self-Government and Territorial Organization of Power in Ukraine, remain incomplete in the ratio of powers and compliance with their financial and economic capacity.

It is significant that in the stages of reform, one of the first steps is to "introduce, as a matter of priority, changes to the Constitution of Ukraine regarding the formation of executive bodies of regional and district councils and the distribution of powers between them".[89] Article 140 of the Constitution of Ukraine establishes that district and regional councils are "bodies of local self-government that represent the common interests of territorial communities of villages, towns, and cities" (a similar meaning is laid down in Article 5 of the Law of Ukraine "On Local Self-Government in Ukraine").[90,91] This means that district and regional councils do

---

88 Організація співробітництва територіальних громад в Україні: практичний посібник для посадових осіб місцевого самоврядування. Київ, 2017. 105 с. URL: https://decentralization.gov.ua/uploads/library/file/11/Organizatsiya-spivrobitnitstva-teritorialnih-gromad-v-Ukrayini.pdf
89 Концепція реформування місцевого самоврядування та територіальної організації влади в Україні від 01.04.2014 р. *Законодавство України*. URL: https://zakon.rada.gov.ua/laws/show/333-2014-%D1%80#Text
90 Конституція України (від 28.06.1996 р. зі змінами). *Президент України*: Офіційне інтернет-представництво. URL: https://www.president.gov.ua/ua/documents/constitution/konstituciya-ukrayini-rozdil-xi
91 Закон Закон України «Про місцеве самоврядування в Україні» від 21.05.1997 р. (зі змінами). *Законодавство України*. URL: https://zakon.rada.gov.ua/laws/show/280/97-%D0%B2%D1%80#Text

not have their own territorial communities and are rather specific representative bodies of local self-government. In the conditions when the majority of powers were transferred from the district level to the level of territorial communities, regional councils gradually began to perform the function of mediator between district councils and united territorial communities, primarily in matters of transfer of disputed property – objects of social, medical or cultural infrastructure, the repairs or construction of which were financed district councils without analyzing the need for these services[92] [193]. At the same time, the probability of regional and district conflicts in the context of the distribution of powers is minimal, which can be visualized in the table.

Taking into account the priority of compliance with the principle of decentralization, it is important to resolve the conflicts that have arisen at the local level without the dominance of the participation of the center. In our opinion, deepening the communication of regional and district councils on solving common issues of exercising powers and optimizing their material and financial component will globally contribute to the harmonization of the entire system of local self-government. At the local level, overcoming at the stage of approval of the reform the consequences of the existing dualism of power at the regional level, when the corresponding state administrations subordinate to the executive branch of government function together with the district and regional councils. As noted by lawyer Y. Buglak, the model of the organization of power at the local and regional levels enshrined in the Constitution of Ukraine is archaic from today's point of view. This model does not fully comply with European standards and the principles of the European Charter of Local Self-Government: the introduction of local self-government takes place only at the territorial level – the level of a settlement (village, town, city), and at the regional level (district, region) there remains a centralized system of direct state administration.[93]

---

92 Проблеми перерозподілу повноважень між районним та базовим рівнями місцевого самоврядування в сучасних умовах: аналітична записка. *Національний інститут стратегічних досліджень*. 2021. URL: https://niss.gov.ua/sites/default/files/2021-08/pererozpodil-povnovazen.pdf

93 Буглак Ю. Проблеми розмежування повноважень між органами виконавчої влади і органами місцевого самоврядування в Україні. *Підприємництво, господарство і право*. 2018. № 11. С. 70–75.

Opportunities to harmonize relations between communities and to satisfy common needs through the establishment of contractual relations are quite broad and institutionally ensured. However, this fact does not prevent the occurrence of conflict situations between UTCs, which mainly concern the establishment of territorial boundaries, financial issues and the field of social protection of the population. The process of creating united territorial communities was conflictual: communities were united artificially, and resources were not always distributed transparently. Relations between the district level and the UTC often became the subject of conflict. There were cases of layering of the conflict between the religious community and the newly united territorial one. Conflicts were caused by unsoldered lands, landfills for solid waste and even cemeteries. The subjects of the conflict can be not only administrative bodies or official officials in communities or councils as a whole but also the public.

The following factors can be an obstacle to community cooperation:
- insufficient level of competence of territorial community leaders and local self-government officials, which negatively affects not only the unification initiative itself but also significantly reduces the expected effectiveness of cooperation;
- large disproportionality of the budgets of territorial communities, which creates risks for more capable communities when combining efforts with less capable or depressed communities;
- risks of the leadership of the territorial community (local elite) regarding the loss of significant influence on decision-making processes in the case of cooperation of several territorial communities, and, as a result, fear of losing influence on the processes of communal property management and distribution of the revenue part of the local budget;
- low involvement of state authorities and local self-governments at the district and regional level in the processes of organizing the cooperation of territorial communities;
- insufficient level of development of local initiatives originating from civil society institutions created in territorial communities;
- low legal and managerial culture of local officials, which be-

comes an obstacle to the development of effective directions and forms of cooperation and their contractual design.[94]

Ways out of the listed situations are unlikely to lie in the legislation; however, objective court decisions, timely qualified mediation of conflicts and the way of contractual resolution of problems can be a solution while the country is going through a trial period of decentralization and restarting the system of local self-government.

The globalization context and the implementation of European integration practices led to attention to the possibilities of cooperation of similar institutional forms of different states of the world, in fact, communities in Ukraine and abroad. As mentioned in the study, local self-governments are legally empowered to conduct international activities.[95] Let's pay attention to older documents: since 1990, Ukraine has concluded more than 800 agreements on trade, economic, scientific, technical and cultural cooperation. The agreements cover all regions and their communities, which have since been linked by contractual partnership relations with the communities of Poland, Lithuania, Estonia, Georgia, the Czech Republic, Bulgaria, Israel, Latvia, Germany, Greece, Croatia, the USA, Canada, Slovakia, Moldova and others of states.[96] In addition to the agreements that established partnerships, friendship and cooperation, there were also those that specified the authority to carry out joint activities in the communal sphere; cross-border trade; environmental protection; scientific, technical and humanitarian issues; protection of cultural heritage, etc.

Territorial communities can form cross-border cooperation in the form of "Union of Euroregional Cooperation" (UEC) on the territory of the member states of the Council of Europe. The purpose of the Euroregional cooperation association is to encourage, sup-

---

94 Сірик З. Проблеми та можливості співробітництва територіальних громад України. *Інвестиції: практика та досвід*. 2017. № 16. С. 102–107.

95 Закон України «Про місцеве самоврядування в Україні» від 21.05.1997 р. (зі змінами). *Законодавство України*. URL: https://zakon.rada.gov.ua/laws/show/280/97-%D0%B2%D1%80#Text

96 Реєстр міжрегіональних угод про торговельно-економічне, науково-технічне і культурне співробітництво. *Міністерство розвитку громад та територій України: Офіційний вебсайт*. URL: https://www.minregion.gov.ua/napryamki-diyalnosti/derzhavna-rehional-na-polityka/mizhregionalne-ta-transkordonne-spivrobitnitstv/reyestr-mizhregionalnih-ugod-pro-torgovelno-ekonomichne-naukovo-tehnichne-i-kulturne-spivrobitnitstvo/

port and develop in the interests of the population cross-border and interterritorial cooperation between its members in areas of common competence and in accordance with the powers established with the national legislation of the respective states.[97]

Regarding Ukrainian legislation, let's refer to the Law "On Transborder Cooperation" dated June 24, 2004.[98] Its goal is the formation of good-neighborly relations and the deepening of interaction between subjects and participants of cross-border cooperation, which contributes to the joint solution of local and regional development tasks. Interaction based on such principles as respect for the internal affairs of states, human rights and their fundamental freedoms, state sovereignty, territorial integrity and inviolability of state borders, mutually beneficial cooperation, taking into account the powers of subjects and the rights of participants in cross-border cooperation when concluding agreements on cross-border cooperation, agreed elimination of political, economic, legal, administrative and other obstacles to mutual cooperation. It is important that the specified Law includes executive bodies of local self-government and structural subdivisions of local executive bodies among the bodies of cross-border cooperation. That is, there is another direction of functional interactions of local self-governments. Structures that carry out general coordination of cross-border cooperation in various fields are Euroregions, European Unions of Territorial Cooperation (EUTC) and Unions of Euroregional Cooperation (EUC).

As the political scientist G. Agafonova points out in her research, since the signing of the political, and especially the economic, part of the Association Agreement between Ukraine and the countries of the European Union, the attention of the regions has been focused on issues of foreign investment, donor aid, grants from EU institutions, etc. The investment attractiveness of communities has become part of their development strategies, and its level is often associated with the promotion of the course of European integra-

---

97 Тимченко І. Територіальна громада у транскордонному просторі: чинники, закономірності, пріоритети розвитку: монографія. Львів: ДУ «Інститут регіональних досліджень імені М. І. Долішнього НАН України», 2019. 444 с.

98 Закон України «Про транскордонне співробітництво» від 24.06.2004 р. *Верховна Рада України*: Офіційний вебсайт. URL: https://zakon.rada.gov.ua/laws/show/1861-15#Text

tion of Ukraine.[99] Usually, scientists describe the investment potential, defining it as a set of investment resources in combination with opportunities, means and conditions for their attraction and use (O. Shcherbatiuk)[100]. The investment potential of a territorial community is a set of resources and opportunities (natural resource, social, financial-economic, institutional-management, etc.), which are the object of management by the authorities of the territorial community, aimed at attracting investment resources to solve the problems of territorial development (P. Zhuk, Z. Siryk)[101]. The investment attractiveness of mountain UTCs is a comprehensive indicator, which reflects a set of investment-significant criteria taking into account the weight of their influence according to the following components: economic, socio-economic, natural resource and infrastructural potentials, taking into account the peculiarities of the state regulatory and legal support for the functioning of mountain UTCs, which is the basis for the formation of a favorable investment environment (I. Andreychuk).[102]

According to the National Bank of Ukraine, at the end of 2021, direct investments in Ukraine exceeded USD 62 billion. Compared to 2015, the volume of direct investment decreased only in Odesa, Cherkasy and Kharkiv regions, and about 70 % of such financing came from the countries of the European Union.[103]

It is already possible to talk about the priority and working areas of investment attraction in communities – energy efficiency and industrial parks. There are also clear rules for the UTC: to create a regime of assistance for the investor, to perceive it as

99 Агафонова Г., Ірха К. Внутрішній і зовнішній виміри співробітництва територіальних громад в Україні. *Вісник Національного технічного університету України «Київський політехнічний інститут». Серія «Політологія. Соціологія. Право».* 2022. № 4. С. 42–50.

100 Щербатюк О. Дефініція «інвестиційний потенціал підприємства»: сутність та відмінності. Ефективна економіка. 2011. № 11. URL: http://www.economy.nayka.com.ua/?op=1&z=773.

101 Жук П., Сірік З. Інвестиційний потенціал територіальних громад: суть поняття та питання управління. *Регіональна економіка.* 2017. № 2. С. 16–22.

102 Андрейчук І., Конкольняк М. Оцінювання інвестиційної привабливості об'єднаних територіальних громад у гірських регіонах на основі державного регулювання. *Економіка та суспільство.* 2021. № 27. URL: https://economyandsociety.in.ua/index.php/journal/article/view/454/436

103 Прямі іноземні інвестиції в регіони України. *VoxUkraine.* 2022. URL: https://voxukraine.org/pryami-inozemni-investytsiyi-v-regiony-ukrayiny/

a desirable partner, to organize all the documentation of the UTC, to develop an appropriate investment strategy, etc. In general, the state has created political and legal conditions for investment, and these are the Laws of Ukraine "On Investment Activity"[104], "On the protection of foreign investments in Ukraine"[105] and "On making changes to some legislative acts of Ukraine regarding the simplification of investment attraction and the introduction of new financial instruments"[106], as well as the clarification of the Ministry of Justice regarding investment legislation.[107] At the same time, no guarantees have been created for local self-government, primarily because the legislation limits their subjectivity in the formation of relations with investors, as it only briefly mentions communities and their official representatives in the listed laws.

The phase of the full-scale invasion of the Russian Federation on the territory of Ukraine, which began on February 24, 2022, affected the format of international cooperation at the regional level. If earlier it was about local cultural, educational, informational and humanitarian projects, environmental initiatives, days of good-neighborliness, etc., now the context of deepening such interactions is completely subordinated to the needs and problems of war. It is about specific types of assistance that Ukraine and its refugees receive. The rhetoric of diplomatic communications has also undergone changes: the position of not only the governments of countries but also individual officials and representatives of communities has appeared. Russian aggression led to the cancellation of sister city status for settlements of the aggressor country. As of April 2022, more than 150 cities in the world have already severed relations with Russian sister cities. Cities in such countries

---

104 Закон України «Про інвестиційну діяльність» від 18.09.1991 р. *Верховна Рада України*: Офіційний вебсайт. URL: https://zakon.rada.gov.ua/laws/show/1560-12#Text

105 Закон України «Про захист іноземних інвестицій на Україні» від 10.09.1991 р. *Верховна Рада України*: Офіційний вебсайт. URL: https://zakon.rada.gov.ua/laws/show/1540%D0%B0-12#Text

106 Закон України «Про внесення змін до деяких законодавчих актів України щодо спрощення залучення інвестицій та запровадження нових фінансових інструментів» від 19.06.2020 р. *Верховна Рада України*: Офіційний вебсайт. URL: https://zakon.rada.gov.ua/laws/show/738-20#Text

107 Інвестиційне законодавство: стан, проблеми, перспективи: Роз'яснення Міністерства юстиції України від 8.05.2012 р. *Верховна Рада України*: Офіційний вебсайт. URL: https://zakon.rada.gov.ua/laws/show/n0015323-12#Text

as Australia, Austria, Great Britain, Denmark, Greece, Estonia, Spain, Italy, Canada, Latvia, Lithuania, Germany, Norway, Peru, Poland, Portugal, Slovakia, Slovenia, USA, Finland and other countries have adopted the corresponding decision.[108]

Ukraine appeals to the principles of self-government of the regions of the partner states so that the local self-governments of the whole world unite their efforts and require the politicians of each country to make tough decisions that would help stop Russian aggression, stop and punish the war crimes that Russia continues to commit in Ukraine. In particular, the Minister of Development of Communities and Territories of Ukraine, O. Chernyshov, appealed to the international community with this appeal. Ukraine voices local demands – to participate in the release of captive representatives of local self-government, to end partnership relations with Russian sister cities, as well as nationwide calls – to close the sky over Ukraine, strengthen economic sanctions against the aggressor country, increase the amount of weapons provided to Ukraine, etc.

Today's realities have changed the format of cooperation between Ukrainian cities and foreign sister cities and partner cities. In the conditions of war, cooperation as a political institution is based on previously concluded bilateral agreements. It implements humanitarian missions from region to region.[109,110]

Close contacts and long-term partnerships of Ukrainian cities not only provided support to their regions but also contributed to attracting appropriate resources to the cities and regions most affected by Russian shelling, serving as a coordination headquarters and transit zone for rubber cargoes. Today, requests for help from sister cities for Ukrainian regions have been specified, as well as an explanation of the possibilities of implementing such help. It

108 Понад 150 міст у світі вже розірвали відносини з російськими містами-побратимами. *Децентралізація*: Офіційний вебпортал.2022. URL: https://decentralization.gov.ua/news/14999
109 Українським громадам допомагають європейські міста-побратими. *Асоціація міст України*: Офіційний вебсайт. 2022. URL: https://auc.org.ua/novyna/ukrayinskym-gromadam-dopomagayut-yevropeyski-mista-pobratymy
110 План реалізації Стратегії розвитку Білокуракинської об'єднаної територіальної громади 2020-2022 рр. *Білокуракинська громада*: Офіційний вебсайт. 2022. URL: https://bilokurakynska-gromada.gov.ua/strategichnij-plan-stalogo-rozvitku-bilokurakinskoi-selischnoi-teritorialnoi-gromadi-do-2026-roku-13-54-37-09-12-2016/

is about the need for post-war reconstruction of settlements, infrastructure, educational, medical and cultural institutions, etc. Prime Minister of Ukraine D. Shmyhal called on the mayors of European and other cities around the world to join in the reconstruction.[111]

According to the Association of Cities of Ukraine, more than 100 Ukrainian cities have about 700 sister cities, and this number is growing even during the war.[112,113]

Regarding the formats, how interaction with sister cities can be established, and what areas of cooperation can be counted on, we will single out the most popular:

- a request for help with a simultaneous invitation to representatives of local authorities to visit a de-occupied city or a city affected by Russian armed aggression. The visits of world leaders and high-ranking officials to Ukraine during the war, through visualization of its consequences, contribute to a real understanding of the affairs and needs of our state and its communities;
- argumentation of support for several areas of necessary assistance at once: for internally displaced persons who are in the territory of Ukraine, and those who are forced to go abroad, primarily to sister cities; for other regions of the country most affected by the war; for relocated enterprises and businesses as important subjects of economic stabilization;
- a call to foreign local governments with the demand to turn to the governments of their countries regarding the provision of military and deepening diplomatic support to Ukraine, increased sanctions pressure on the Russian Federation, etc.;
- formation and filling of the counter-propaganda segment through communication with foreign communities, business, public opinion leaders, media, creation of information drives about Ukraine.

We can point out the successful start of cooperation with the

---

111 Як міста-побратими можуть допомогти у відновленні України? Приклади та інструкція. *Рубрика.* 2022. URL: https://rubryka.com/article/twin-cities-help-ukraine/
112 Громади, НЕ МОВЧІТЬ! У вас сотні міст-побратимів. Зверніться до них за підтримкою. *Децентралізація*: Офіційний вебпортал. 2022. URL: https://decentralization.gov.ua/news/14626
113 Токвіль А. Про демократію в Америці. Київ: Видавничий дім «Всесвіт», 1999. 590 с.

involvement of sister cities, friendly states and their regions in the post-war reconstruction of Ukrainian settlements and current projects in de-occupied cities, villages and towns.

Due to the challenges of the martial law, the assessment of international cooperation at the regional level has changed. Its meaning became concrete; its effectiveness became more obvious. Some foreign regions share their experience, others advocate for Ukraine at a higher state level, others unceasingly send humanitarian cargo to our country, others provide treatment and rehabilitation of our wounded civilians and soldiers, and some combine all the above functions and all together support our refugees. It is clear that the idea of twin cities is evolving, its current concept dates back to the end of the Second World War, which means that it has not been tested by large-scale military events.

The Russian-Ukrainian war stimulated the established fraternity to move from rhetoric to action, from conceptuality to concreteness and from support to direct assistance. And these aspects equally affected the format of relations between twin cities and partner cities.

Summing up, let's emphasize the urgency of expanding the boundaries of perception of cooperation between communities. Outside of the new legislation, we will continue to consider communities as residents of each specific settlement, who can jointly implement various meaningful interactions, including with foreign institutions, communities, etc. Approvingly evaluating the conditions created for the cooperation of the UTCs within the country, we emphasize the need for a comprehensive addition to the institutional plane for the development and deepening of international contacts of communities with regard to attracting investments and other donor assistance, implementing joint projects with sister cities, and strengthening the political and legal subjectivity of territorial communities in the context of participation in international relations, in particular cross-border relations. These aspects become especially important in the conditions of widespread mobilization of the world community in support of Ukraine in the fight against Russian military aggression.

Distribution of powers of local self-governments at the regional and district levels[114]

The regional level (oblast)	District level (rayon)
– regional development; – environmental protection; – development of regional infrastructure, primarily regional highways, public transport routes; – professional and technical education; – providing highly specialized medical assistance; – development of culture, sports, tourism.	– education and training of children in boarding schools; – providing secondary level medical services.

114 Концепція реформування місцевого самоврядування та територіальної організації влади в Україні від 01.04.2014 р. *Законодавство України.* URL: https://zakon.rada.gov.ua/laws/show/333-2014-%D1%80#Text

PART 6

**Problems and Risks of Reforming
the Territorial Organization
of Government**

On April 1, 2014, Ukraine approved the Concept of Reform of Local Self-Government and Territorial Organization of Power. From this date, a new stage of formation of an effective system of regional governance begins. The processes are subject to the reform of decentralization of power, the purpose of which is to transfer powers, including financial ones, and resources from state power as close as possible to people, that is, to local self-government bodies. It is clear that this increases the responsibility of local self-government bodies, which must simultaneously carry out organizational work in communities and acquire new experience in administrative management.

The purpose of the Concept of Local Self-Government Reform and Territorial Organization of Power was to determine the directions, mechanisms and terms of the formation of effective local self-government and territorial organization of power to create and maintain a full-fledged living environment for citizens, provide high-quality and accessible public services, establish institutions of direct people's power, satisfy the interests of citizens in all areas of life in the relevant territory and coordinate the interests of the state and territorial communities. Achieving the goal and overcoming existing problems was planned by the following steps:

- determination of the territorial basis for local self-governments and executive authorities capable of ensuring the availability and proper quality of public services provided by such bodies, as well as the necessary resource base;
- creation of appropriate material, financial and organizational conditions to ensure the implementation by local self-governments of their own and delegated powers;
- separation of powers in the system of local self-governments and executive bodies at different levels of the administrative-territorial system according to the principle of subsidiarity;
- separation of powers between executive authorities and local self-governments on the basis of decentralization of power;
- introduction of a mechanism of state control over the conformity of decisions of local self-governments with the Constitution and laws of Ukraine and the quality of public services provision to the population;
- maximum involvement of the population in making manage-

ment decisions, promoting the development of forms of direct popular government;
- improvement of the mechanism of coordination of activities of local executive bodies.[115]

The document also determined that the formation of criteria for administrative-territorial units of different levels of the administrative-territorial system of the state is carried out taking into account three levels of the administrative-territorial system:
1. basic (administrative-territorial units – communities);
2. district (administrative-territorial units – districts);
3. regional (administrative-territorial units – Autonomous Republic of Crimea, oblasts, cities Kyiv and Sevastopol).

The territory of the administrative-territorial unit had to be inseparable, and within the boundaries of the administrative-territorial unit, there could not be other administrative-territorial units of the same level. The territory of the administrative-territorial unit of the basic level was determined taking into account the availability of basic public services provided on the territory of the community.

The main aspects of the change in the territorial organization of power in Ukraine are:
- legal – development of new and improvement of the current legislation, which regulates the decentralization reform;
- economic – the relationship between the implementation of the specified reform and the economic development of the country and vice versa;
- social – refers to the focus of decentralization on meeting people's social needs;
- organizational – includes a step-by-step process of reform, which is aimed at creating capable local self-government bodies.[116]

The construction of the national model of the territorial organization of power, starting from 2014, is taking place quite quickly

115 Про схвалення Концепції реформування місцевого самоврядування та територіальної організації влади в Україні від 01.04.2014 р. *Законодавство України.*URL: https://zakon.rada.gov.ua/laws/show/Text
116 Про схвалення Концепції реформування місцевого самоврядування та територіальної організації влади в Україні від 01.04.2014 р. *Законодавство України.*URL: https://zakon.rada.gov.ua/laws/show/333-2014-%D1%80#Text

and noticeably. First of all, this is justified by the change in the boundaries of territorial formations, the number of districts, and the content of the territorial community. In June 2020, the Cabinet of Ministers of Ukraine approved a new administrative-territorial system of the basic level, which is represented by 1,469 territorial communities. Already in July of the same year, the Verkhovna Rada of Ukraine adopted a resolution on reducing the number of districts (rayons) – from 490 to 136. The territories of the new districts consist of rural, township and urban territorial communities. In October 2020, the first local elections were held in Ukraine on the new territorial basis of communities and districts.

Government and parliamentary decisions adopted in 2020 made it possible to scale up decentralization processes throughout the country, complete the process of creating capable communities, and implement new administrative zoning of the country. The foundation of the reform, which Ukraine has been working on for more than six years, is the basis for building a qualitatively new system of local self-government bodies. At the same time, the role of the districts was changing. The head of the district state administration was supposed to become a representative of the central government with supervisory functions. Districts are needed primarily for the organization of territorial subdivisions of state authorities. These steps were important for the cohesion of the state, because each new territorial community became a new link in the "center-region" chain.[117]

Currently, the territorial organization of the authorities has solved the tasks of defining territories, their borders and sizes. The next relevant aspect is the power aspect, that is, the authority of these territorial units. And even if there were fewer districts, the district level of self-government remained. Now Ukraine needs to specify and delimit the powers of regional, district, city, village and village councils.

The issue of normalizing the activity of district-level councils is really acute because their powers and financial capacity are currently characterized as disproportionate, in particular, due to the fact that the districts "inherited" common communal property,

---

117 Гоголь Т., Мельничук Л. Трансформація територіальних громад в умовах децентралізації в Україні. *Право та державне управління*. 2022. № 1. С. 225.

which must be transferred to newly created communities, which, in turn, are not required by law to accept this property. If there is no coordination of interests, the districts must maintain the facilities at the expense of non-existent funding at this level. This is one of the contradictions that are at the stage of regulatory settlement.

According to researchers T. Gogol and L. Melnychuk, the biggest risks of current reforms in Ukraine are related to the existence and accumulation of institutional, resource and socio-demographic barriers, which should be taken into account during the development and implementation of specific community development mechanisms. In particular, the issue of the distribution of powers and budget funds in the conditions of the new zoning is unresolved. It is necessary to implement a set of measures to minimize the risks of the process of changes in the administrative-territorial structure of the sub-regional level in ensuring the provision of services provided at the district level. They require regulatory changes and monitoring of the interaction of state authorities and local self-government, synchronization of the development of territorial levels of the economy in conditions of decentralization. After all, executive power at the regional and district levels is exercised by local state administrations, which limits the independence of councils and mixes the functions of the state and local self-government.[118]

Local self-government experts constantly identify new gaps in the legislative regulation of the functioning of representative and executive bodies of local self-government. Most of them are due to the fact that the majority of basic-level units do not confirm the presence of sufficient economic potential for their development. At the same time, it has been proven that viable territorial-administrative entities must have high financial and economic, institutional and personnel potential to ensure the proper level of providing services to the population and socio-economic progress. A separate problem is the gradual degradation of the rural settlement system and the accelerated depopulation of small rural communities.

---

118 Гоголь Т., Мельничук Л. Трансформація територіальних громад в умовах децентралізації в Україні. *Право та державне управління*. 2022. № 1. С. 222.

As the researcher of the Institute of Demography and Social Research named after M. V. Ptukh O. Dyakonenko notes, even under the conditions of increasing the financial and economic potential of rural settlements, the migration outflow of residents to cities and related processes of depopulation of the rural population will continue. Due to the low rate of formation of the UTC, the rural population in the Kyiv and Kharkiv regions migrated intensively, which, in turn, weakened the productive impact of the reform on the preservation of human potential within the territorial community. Urbanization processes and depopulation of the rural population, caused primarily by the low standard of living in rural areas, the deficit of the rural budget and limited resource potential, can be minimized by using the advantages provided by the administrative-territorial reform and implementing the latest strategic directions of development.[119]

Options for solving the problem are described in the current documents – the Concept for the Development of Rural Areas from 2015 and the Concept for Stimulating the Development of Entrepreneurship in Rural Areas from 2021.[120] The purpose of the 2015 Concept is to create the necessary organizational, legal and financial prerequisites for rural development by:
- diversification of economic activity;
- increasing the level of real income from agricultural and non-agricultural activities in the village;
- achieving guaranteed social standards and improving the living conditions of the rural population;
- environmental protection, preservation and restoration of natural resources in rural areas;
- preservation of the rural population as a bearer of Ukrainian identity, culture and spirituality;

119 Дяконенко О. Розвиток сільських поселень в умовах адміністративно-територіальної реформи. *Матеріали Міжнародної науково-практичної конференції «Адміністративно-територіальні vs економічно-просторові кордони регіонів»*. 2020. URL:
120 Концепція розвитку сільських територій від 23.09.2015 р. *Верховна Рада України*: Офіційний вебсайт. URL: https://zakon.rada.gov.ua/laws/show/995-2015-Text; Концепція стимулювання розвитку підприємництва на сільських територіях до 2030 року. *Міністерство аграрної політики та продовольства України: Офіційний вебсайт*. 2021. URL: https://minagro.gov.ua/npa/pro-shvalennya-koncepciyi-stimuly-uvannya-rozvitku-pidpriyemnictva-na-silskih-teritoriyah-do-2030-roku

– creation of conditions for expanding the opportunities of territorial communities of villages and settlements to solve their existing problems;
– bringing legislation in the field of rural development into compliance with EU standards.[121]

The document of 2021 refers to the comprehensive development of villages, aimed at stable provision of the rise of agricultural production, rural entrepreneurship, improvement of working and living conditions of the population, preservation of the environment, restoration and sustainable use of natural resources, which should become the key to the development of the country's agrarian sector.[122]

In fact, the problem of the number of the rural population is confirmed primarily by statistical data. According to the State Statistics Service, in relation to the urban population, the rural population in Ukraine was in:

– 1990–2000 – 32 %;
– 2010 – 31 %;
– 2020 – 30 %.[123]

Experts in demography note that taking into account the rate of internal migration, the real ratio differs significantly from official statistics, and not in favor of the rural population. Thus, the reason for this situation lies not only in the influence of administrative and territorial transformations in the country.

In 2022, another important phenomenon for the state, which is related to administrative units, occurred in Ukraine. This is the activation of national resistance in the form of territorial defense a system of nationwide, military and special measures carried out in peacetime and in special periods with the aim of countering military threats, as well as providing assistance in the protection

---

121 Концепція розвитку сільських територій від 23.09.2015 р. *Верховна Рада України*: Офіційний вебсайт. URL: https://zakon.rada.gov.ua/laws/show/995-2015-Text
122 Концепція стимулювання розвитку підприємництва на сільських територіях до 2030 року. *Міністерство аграрної політики та продовольства України:Офіційний вебсайт*. 2021. URL: https://minagro.gov.ua/npa/pro-shvalennya-koncepciyi-stimulyuvannya-rozvitku-pidpriyemnictva-na-silskih-teritoriyah-do-2030-roku
123 Монолатій І., Великочий В., Плекан Ю. «Були трактовані наскрізь гуманно...». Косачівський табір для інтерованих осіб в контексті українсько-польських взаємин у Галичині (1918–1919 рр.): колективна монографія. Івано-Франківськ: Видавець Кушнір Г. М., 2019. 182 с.

of the population, territories, the environment and property from extraordinary situations. According to the Law "On the Basics of National Resistance", the territorial defense district defines a part of the land territory of Ukraine, which is included in the territory of the corresponding zone of territorial defense of Ukraine and whose borders coincide with the administrative boundaries of the district within the Autonomous Republic of Crimea, the region, the cities of Kyiv, Sevastopol.[124]

Although the organization and execution of territorial defense tasks belong to the Territorial Defense Forces as a component of the Armed Forces of Ukraine, the preparation of Ukrainian citizens for national resistance is carried out by state bodies and local self-government bodies. Voluntary formations of territorial communities are formed taking into account the resource and human capabilities of the respective local authorities. The subject of territorial defense created in a specific UTC can perform its duties in any region of the country; it is not a local army for the protection of territories. In the conditions of the war, Territorial Defense Units became an integral part of the responsibility of administrative-territorial units – local self-government bodies, directly residents of communities.

Until February 24, 2022, it could be argued that two important processes are taking place in the political sphere of Ukraine at the same time: European integration as a course for rapprochement with the European Union with the aim of further accession and decentralization – granting a significant amount of powers to communities, which is also inextricably linked to the direction of European integration. After all, compliance with the principle of subsidiarity is among the leading conditions for reforming local self-government and territorial organization of power in Ukraine, and this is the main feature of the interaction of all levels of government in Europe. The newest and unprecedented challenge for all political institutions and processes connected with them was the full-scale war of the Russian Federation against Ukraine, its independence, sovereignty, rights and freedoms of citizens. Under

---

124 Закон України «Про основи національного спротиву» від 16.07.2021 р. *Верховна Рада України*: Офіційний вебсайт. URL: https://zakon.rada.gov.ua/laws/show/1702-20#Text

such conditions, it is quite difficult to carry out the applied aspect of the study of the administrative-territorial system, approbation of the reform, because part of the territories remain temporarily occupied by the enemy.

Summarizing the scientific research presented in the emphasis, we state the problems in reforming the territorial organization of power in Ukraine:

- there is still a need to specify and delimit the powers of councils at different levels, especially in the case when the boundaries of the district coincide with the boundaries of the united territorial community;
- the probability of inconsistency of personnel, material, technical and financial resources with the received amount of property, which was transferred to the management of the community. Such problems are more often faced by the district level, whose financial powers do not correspond to property obligations;
- problems of rural areas – a gradual depopulation of the population of small rural communities is observed;
- the inconsistency of the legislation, intervention in which does not seem to solve the problems that arise, but deepens them. In our opinion, the reason for this lies in the lack of constructive communication, which should accompany the entire process of territorial reorganization and include all interested parties (parliamentarians, government officials, experts, etc.).

PART 7

**Prospects for the Integration
of European Experience into the System
of Local Self-government of Ukraine
and the Format of the Territorial
Organization of Power**

The process of European integration is a vector for the introduction of systemic reforms, determined by the general vision of the state's development and the constitutionally defined goal of Ukraine's accession to the European Union. Guidelines for changes in the exercise of power and the implementation of people's power are laid down in the provisions of the Agreement on the Association of Ukraine and the EU. However, it will not be possible to link the local self-government reform, in particular, its decentralization component, with the specified document, since it is not mentioned or specified in the Agreement. These aspects correspond to the principles recognized by the parties to the Agreement:

- respect for democratic values;
- rule of law, good governance, human rights and fundamental freedoms;
- respect for diversity, human dignity and commitment to the principles of a free market economy, which contribute to Ukraine's participation in European policies;
- stability and effectiveness of democratic institutions, etc.

We also emphasize the important points of the "Agenda of the association between Ukraine and the EU for the preparation and promotion of the implementation of the Association Agreement" dated March 16, 2015, which refers to such priorities as:

- introducing amendments to the Constitution for the decentralization of power;
- strengthening the functioning of local and creating regional self-government, the legal status of service in local self-government bodies, in particular through decentralization, which will grant them significant powers and provide financial resources in accordance with the relevant standards contained in the European Charter of Local Self-Government.[125]

During the ratification, the fact that it was carried out without any reservations on the part of Ukraine became indicative. However, this approach of the parliament led to an almost constant conflict between Ukraine and the Council of Europe, since neither

---

125 Порядок денний асоціації між Україною та ЄС для підготовки та сприяння імплементації Угоди про асоціацію. *Урядовий портал*.URL: https://www.kmu.gov.ua/storage/app/imported_content/news/doc_248012532/UA_15-1%20final.pdf

politically nor legally our state could fulfill the obligations of the Charter for a long time. Therefore, in the process of reform, the state periodically asked questions about how Ukraine's international obligations in the field of local self-government would be fulfilled. Analysis of the principles provided by the Charter of local self-government (primarily democracy and decentralization of power) shows that modern Europe sees local self-government as an extremely important element of democracy. It is about reducing the role of the state to the necessary minimum, limiting bureaucratic pressure on the part of officials, which helps attract people to the values of people's rule. The experience of self-management, and most importantly, the skills developed by it, instill in the population a sense of civic responsibility for making decisions about local development.[126] The problems of implementation of the principles of the Charter of local self-government at the current stage are determined, firstly, by the reform of local self-government and the need to form a normative and legal basis for such reform, taking into account modern international standards; secondly, the need to develop organizational and legal mechanisms for the implementation of the provisions of the Additional Protocol to the European Charter of Local Self-Government on the right to participate in local government affairs.[127]

Despite the convincing steps in the implementation of the decentralization reform, the question of its constitutional consolidation remains open. Currently, no changes have been made to the Constitution that would ensure the irreversibility of the process of decentralization of power and local self-government reform.

Discussions of the problems of self-government always actualize the idea of subsidiarity, which is related to decentralization. Researcher O. Moshak defines this as an organizational and legal principle, according to which tasks should be solved at the lowest or remotest level – where their solution is possible and effective.

126 Мельничук В. Імплементація принципів європейської хартії місцевого самоврядування в контексті децентралізації влади. *Вісник Прикарпатського університету. Серія «Політологія»*. 2019. № 13. С. 111–118.
127 Протокол № 3 до Європейської рамкової конвенції про транскордонне співробітництво між територіальними общинами або властями стосовно об'єднань єврорегіонального співробітництва. *Верховна Рада України*: Офіційний вебсайт. URL: https://zakon.rada.gov.ua/laws/show/994_947#Text

Therefore, the central government should play a subsidiary (supporting) role.[128] We emphasize that the described principle is the basis of the European Charter of Local Self-Government, which states: "[P]ublic powers are exercised mainly by those public authorities that have the closest contact with the citizen. When assigning certain powers to another body, it is necessary to take into account the scope and nature of the task, as well as the requirements for achieving efficiency and economy".[129] That is, the transfer of management functions takes place at the level closest to the population, and the main condition here is the ability to effectively perform the specified functions.

Let us emphasize that decentralization as a popular political slogan is usually characterized by opportunities and prospects, state aid and external financial support. However, its essence is determined by a significant layer of obligations and compliance requirements – the ability to comply with them determines the capacity of united territorial communities. Awareness of this is a stage that the European community has already passed. In fact, the key and most difficult step in Ukrainians' acceptance of European rules is the acceptance of not only rights but also obligations.

The success of the local self-government reform depends not only on political will but also on the understanding and support of the residents of the newly created communities. The level of their awareness, the quality of communication with the authorities – both at the central and regional levels – is also a key to effective socio-political changes. Currently, the results of sociological surveys show that Ukrainians do not feel positive changes from the implementation of the decentralization reform.[130] Under such circumstances, it is appropriate to emphasize the following theses:
-    decentralization is not an external requirement, but one of the

---

128 Монолатій І. Міжгрупові інтеракції в етнополітичному дискурсі: проблеми теорії та методології. Івано-Франківськ: Лілея-НВ, 2011. 191 с.

129 Європейська хартія місцевого самоврядування (м. Страсбург, 15 жовтня 1985 року): офіційний переклад .Законодавство України. URL: https://zakon.rada.gov.ua/laws/show/994_036#Text

130 Громадська думка населення щодо реформи децентралізації та її результатів (серпень 2020 р.). *Фонд «Демократичні ініціативи» ім. Ілька Кучеріва.*URL: https://dif.org.ua/article/gromadska-dumka-naselennya-shchodo-reformi-detsentralizatsii-ta-ii-rezultativ

important democratic principles; it is one of the most effective mechanisms for the inclusion of citizens in the construction of a comfortable environment for their own life;

- the process of involving citizens in the formation of the system of local self-government becomes the key to its transformation into an institution of local democracy. However, only the awareness that democratic principles balance opportunities, rights and responsibilities allows this system to be progressive, self-sufficient and fair;

- European integration is an auxiliary tool for studying and borrowing the best European practices of the functioning of the political system at all levels. Having correctly assessed one's own potential, it is possible to change the previously chosen continental model of local government organization, which gravitates towards centralized management, and to test those models of governance where local communities acquire authority;

- in the conditions of European integration, it is important to emphasize the possibility of direct cooperation and communication of local self-governments and representatives of the public sector of Ukraine with the relevant European institutions. In addition to gaining experience, such interaction will increase the professional level of regional officials and industry activists, and attract various types of investments for the development of communities.[131]

The problem of the relationship between the institution of local self-government and the policy of European integration is usually considered in the context of the demands of the latter to reform the organization of the local government system. Obviously, we are talking about decentralization at all levels as a component of Ukraine's European integration obligations under the Association Agreement with the EU. Even long before the signing of the Agreement, the issue of compliance with the norms and standards of the

---

131 Мельничук В. Євроінтеграційний чинник реформування місцевого самоврядування в Україні. *Перспективи розвитку наукових досліджень у контексті глобалізаційних змін: освіта, політика, економіка, міжкультурна комунікація: Матеріали V міжнар. наук.-практ. конф. (м. Сєвєродонецьк, 8 червня 2021 р.)*. Сєвєродонецьк: Вид-во СНУ ім. В. Даля, 2021. С. 101–105.

European Charter of Local Self-Government, which Ukraine ratified on July 15, 1997, became relevant. Today, the Charter is a part
of national legislation and a key guideline for the functioning of
local self-government.

According to the Agenda of the Association, strengthening the
stability, independence and efficiency of institutions that ensure
compliance with democratic principles and the rule of law involves, firstly, "conducting and completing the process of comprehensive and transparent constitutional reform, including the decentralization of power, taking into account the recommendations
of the Venice Commission"; secondly, "strengthening the functioning of local and creating regional self-government, the legal status
of service in local self-government bodies, in particular through
decentralization in accordance with the relevant standards contained in the European Charter".[132] In our opinion, this argumentation is sufficient to understand one side of the mentioned problem – the place of local self-government in European integration
requirements. Let's try to outline another aspect – the role of the
local self-government system in the implementation of European
standards of self-government, or more generally – all European
integration practices of Ukraine.

Here it is important to emphasize several universal and relevant provisions for modern Ukraine:

1. The local level – the level of communities – is a measure of per-
    ception, assimilation and reproduction potential of any innova-
    tions. It is impossible to evaluate the implementation of modern
    political changes, focusing only on the central level. In Ukraine,
    as in any other state, the "center-periphery" relationship tends
    to the predominance of the center.
2. The democratization of the state is conditioned by the establish-
    ment of parity relations and effective communication between
    the bodies of state power and local self-government. They are
    able to activate the political, economic, social, and cultural de-
    velopment of territorial communities and improve the quality

---

132 Чому децентралізація політичної влади в Україні є завданням європейської
інтеграції? *Євроінтеграційний портал.* URL: https://eu-ua.kmu.gov.ua/analityka/
chomu-decentralizaciya-polytychnoyi-vlady-v-ukrayini-ye-zavdannyam-yevropey-
skoyi

of life of the population (this is emphasized in the Sustainable Development Strategy "Ukraine – 2020").

3. The activity of local self-governments in the implementation of international cooperation is part of the successful implementation of relevant European standards, the exchange of experience in managing the local economy and the management of regional processes in the functioning of communities, deepening the relationship between the state and public sectors at the local level.

The stated theses were confirmed by the example of the Western neighbors, which implemented democratic reforms of local self-government through decentralization (e.g., the already mentioned countries of the Visegrad Group), and relate to modern systemic transformations in Ukraine. In fact, it is about granting real, first of all, budgetary powers to newly created territorial communities, optimizing the electoral process on the ground with the strengthening of the party component, transforming the concept of "capable communities" from a requirement of the government's methodology to an objective characteristic of UTC, etc. These steps are not complete, but already in their structure they have successful cases of governance and organization of activities within the framework of the new administrative-territorial system.

It is possible to compare what European countries paid attention to when implementing their reforming steps during the development of the system of local self-government. An analysis of the results of research by the Open Society Institute of the Baltic countries (Estonia, Latvia, Lithuania) and Central Eastern Europe (CEE) (Poland, Hungary, Slovenia, Slovakia and the Czech Republic) shows that during the introduction of decentralization reforms, the governments of these countries paid considerable attention to such components, as:

- legislative, constitutional base and structure of local authorities;
- local politics, decision-making methods and internal organization;
- management of local authorities and mechanisms for providing services;
- financial issues and financial management;

– market-oriented economic development.[133]

The decentralization process in the system of authorities in the countries of Central and Eastern Europe and the Baltic States was based on the principles "from a system of local state power to a system of local self-government" and "from a strong state to a strong civil society".[134]

– As for the content of these points in Ukraine, from a formal point of view, everything coincides:

– a legislative framework has been created. The structure of local self-governments has been formed and established; a whole chapter is devoted to local self-government in the Constitution, but it still does not guarantee compliance with the principle of decentralization;

– local politics existed in Ukraine even before the reform, its content and powers were determined by separate laws. Subsidiarity did not contribute to an objective assessment of the influence of the local level of politics on the capacity to expand its functions. In fact, this only happened with the introduction of decentralization;

– in Ukraine, there is an extensive system of local affairs management bodies, both self-governing representative bodies elected already on the basis of the new legislation, and representative government local bodies. Expanding the range of administrative services that citizens and institutions will be able to receive in the community is an important task today both for the central government and for the UTC;

– budget decentralization, which began in Ukraine in 2015, is still ongoing. The reform of inter-budgetary relations and changes to tax legislation, in particular, contributed to increasing the level of financial support of local budgets; ensured the formation of new progressive relations in the management of budgetary resources; created conditions for motivating local self-governments to increase the revenue base of local budgets.

---

133 Лелеченко А., Васильєва О., Куйбіда В. Місцеве самоврядування в умовах децентралізації повноважень: навч. посіб. Київ, 2017. 110 с. С. 29

134 Slavinskaite N. The Fiscal Decentralization Initiative for Central and Eastern Europe. *Global Journal of Business Economics and Management Current Issues.* 2017. № 7(1):69. URL: https://www.researchgate.net/publication/316067928_Fiscal_decentralization_in_Central_and_Eastern_Europe

A two-level model of inter-budget relations is being formed in the country, as a result of which almost 900 territorial communities have a new level of budgetary powers and relations with the state budget;[135]

- economic development of communities, focused on market relations – so far there is a formal characteristic of the current stage of decentralization. The state is not an effective mediator of these processes for the communities, and the communities themselves have not adjusted to the goal of self-sufficiency and achieving financial capacity. All these issues are usually equated with the aspect of investments – their attraction, expansion and creation of a favorable investment climate. According to government officials, a positive achievement of the above-mentioned reform of inter-budgetary relations is the annual increase in investment resources of local budgets and the growth of the share of expenditures for the performance of self-government powers.[136]

Europe, while implementing the decentralization reform, reduced the number of municipalities. For example, in the period 1952 1992, such a wave swept through Denmark, Great Britain, Germany, Austria, Norway, and the Netherlands, where the total number of municipalities decreased by 40–80 %. Such consolidation was considered the key to the creation of politically, economically and administratively decentralized structures, where the reduction of the number of bureaucratic entities was supposed to make management decisions faster, more transparent, closer to the end users – the residents of the communities. The same processes, but with a delay of several decades, are also taking place in Ukraine.

As Professor V. Marchuk observes, with respect to the French experience, certain analogies can be drawn with Ukraine in how community/community cooperation occurs and what is stimulated. The French authorities in every possible way motivate the

---

135 Улютін Д. Бюджетна децентралізація: головні виклики та досягнення. Децентралізація: Офіційний вебпортал. 2020. URL: https://decentralization.gov.ua/news/12661
136 Улютін Д. Бюджетна децентралізація: головні виклики та досягнення. *Децентралізація*: Офіційний вебпортал. 2020. URL: https://decentralization.gov.ua/news/12661

communes to cooperate and join forces to solve important issues and tasks in the region. This motivation is usually financial, that is, the state forms projects that communes have to implement jointly. As a result, there is a phenomenon of "commune commune" in the country – an association based on the principle of a common goal. In Ukraine, on the other hand, a regulatory basis has been created so that the local community organizations themselves can implement common aspirations and projects, attract external funding, and solve tasks important for several united communities (opening of the National Waste Management Center, construction of a road or landfill for solid household waste, etc.). Statistics show that this approach also works.[137]

The issues that cause discussions concern the competences of local self-government bodies, which, despite all the discussions, are still implemented. Studying the relevant European experience, we state that the directions of these competencies in Ukraine coincide with European ones:

- in the field of financial and economic activity: adoption of the local budget, participation in economic and social projects, collection of local taxes and their accumulation;
- in the field of public order protection: in accordance with the Laws of Ukraine "On Local Self-Government" and "On Participation of Citizens in the Protection of Public Order and the State Border", local self-governments and structures subordinate to them are authorized to perform public order protection functions[138,139].
- in the field of communal services, beautification and environmental protection: under the authority of local self-governments, certain sections of roads, other infrastructure facilities, municipal transport, solid waste collection and disposal servic-

137 Мельничук В., Марчук В. Стан інтеграції європейського досвіду у функціонування системи місцевого самоврядування України. *Регіональні студії*. 2022. № 31. С. 117–124.

138 Закон України «Про місцеве самоврядування в Україні» від 21.05.1997 р. (зі змінами). *Законодавство України*. URL: https://zakon.rada.gov.ua/laws/show/280/97-%D0%B2%D1%80#Text

139 Закон України «Про транскордонне співробітництво» від 24.06.2004 р. *Верховна Рада України*: Офіційний вебсайт. URL: https://zakon.rada.gov.ua/laws/show/1861-15#Text

es are functioning. The area of coastal fortifications and anti-flood measures, which are traditionally underfunded by the state and not supported by local budgets, remains problematic;

– in the social sphere: local self-governments, in particular, provide assistance to vulnerable sections of the population, take care of social institutions, keep relevant registers, slowly, but deal with issues of housing provision, maintain and repair communal institutions of education, culture, health care, etc.

The question of forming a national model of local self-government remains open for Ukraine. In our opinion, the perception of it by various experts and officials is disconnected from the real system of relations within local self-government and with the center. Perhaps this is a relevant self-governing model for Ukraine, which may change, evolve, be adjusted by legislation, etc. over time.

The megatrend of modern European municipalism is the principle of sustainable development and strategic orientation, which involves taking into account the interests of future generations. The needs of future generations are taken into account in the current activities of local self-government. Decisions at the local level must take into account all costs, whether environmental, structural, financial, economic or social, in order to prevent the transmission of problems and tensions to future generations. There must be a comprehensive and strategic vision for the future of the local community with an understanding of what is needed for such development.[140] This trend is also a part of the Ukrainian present. The sustainability of territorial development in Ukraine is recognized to be no less important than financial resources. In Ukraine, work continues on updating the legislation on the functioning of local self-government, where, in particular, the norms of the Law of Ukraine "On the Goals of Sustainable Development of Ukraine for the period until 2030" will be implemented.[141]

The starting points of the updated system of local self-government are human capital (85 % of the country's population lives with-

---

140 Про Стратегію сталого розвитку «Україна – 2020». Указ Президента України від 12.01.2015 р. № 5/2015. *Законодавство України*. URL: http://zakon4.rada.gov.ua/laws/show/5/2015

141 Законодавство про децентралізацію. *Децентралізація*: Офіційний вебпортал. URL: https://decentralization.gov.ua/legislations?year=&legislation_ type=&legislation_state=&legislation_topic=&legislation_name=&legislation_number=

in the boundaries of the formed self-government units), huge territories (almost 92 % of the territory of Ukraine is covered by united territorial communities)[142] and the economy of regional markets, transit and cross-border resources (the length of Ukraine's border with EU countries is almost 1,360 km). In the State Regional Development Strategy for 2021–2027, among the competitive advantages of Ukrainian regions, the powerful historical and cultural potential and the affordable cost of living in Ukraine compared to most European countries are also indicated [187]. The same document also lists the challenges that Ukraine has faced at the current stage – from the armed aggression of the Russian Federation, the full-scale stage of which the terrorist country began in February 2022, to the demographic crisis, climate change and the deterioration of the ecological situation.

Summing up, we state that the system of local self-government is one of the main objects of European integration transformations in Ukraine. On the other hand, it has a tangible potential in the implementation of reforms established by the Association Agreement.[143]

Studying and borrowing the experience of European self-governing practices is pervasive for all research issues. In this regard, our vision does not completely coincide with the opinions established in politics and expert circles. Ukraine had several imprudent cases of tracing Western processes and vectors of institutional development, when national peculiarities were not taken into account. As for the deepening of integration, in the conditions of already viable communities, it is possible to give them the authority and the opportunity to expand the toolkit of their activities due to the adaptation of European cases of local democracy and interaction with the population.

The main aspects of the change in the territorial organization of power in Ukraine are defined as legal, economic, social and or-

---

142 *Децентралізація*: Офіційний портал. URL: https://decentralization.gov.ua/new-gromada

143 Мельничук В. Зв'язок системи місцевого самоврядування та реалізації курсу європейської інтеграції України. *Пріоритетні напрями наукових досліджень: філософський, політологічний та культурологічний аспекти: Матеріали міжнародної науково-практичної конференції (м. Київ, 8–9 жовтня 2021 р.)*. Київ: Таврійський національний університет імені В. І. Вернадського, 2021. С. 46–50.

ganizational. The rapid start of the construction of the national model of the territorial organization of power is justified by the change in the boundaries of territorial entities, the number of districts (from 490 to 136), and the content and meaning of the territorial community. Government and parliamentary decisions adopted in 2020 made it possible to scale up decentralization processes throughout the country, complete the process of creating capable communities and implement new administrative zoning of the country.

It was found that the problems of reforming the territorial organization of power in Ukraine are the existing need to specify and delimit the powers of councils of different levels, the possibility of a mismatch of personnel, material, technical, and financial resources of the UTC to the amount of property obtained, problems of rural areas, inconsistencies in legislation and communication dysfunction in the relations of participants' administrative and territorial reform and interested parties.

European integration is defined as an auxiliary tool for studying and borrowing the best European practices of the functioning of the political system at all levels. It is emphasized that, having correctly assessed one's own potential, it is possible to modify the previously chosen continental model of local government organization, which gravitates towards centralized management, and to test those models of governance where local communities acquire authority.

It was established that the system of local self-government, on the one hand, is one of the main objects of European integration transformations in Ukraine; on the other hand, it has a tangible potential in the implementation of reforms established by the Agreement on the Association of Ukraine and the countries of the European Union. Regarding decentralization and reformatting of the territorial-administrative system, we have stable starting positions that are sufficiently correlated with European norms and proven practices of European countries.

Conclusions

The monograph analyzes the forms of administrative transfer of powers and decentralization of power and proves the evolutionary nature of the development of theories of local self-government. The self-governing subjectivity of territories is analyzed as the ability to organize the social life of the local population and ensure economic distribution in accordance with the current hierarchy in society. The authors see the institutionalization of local self-government as a mandatory element of the political system, an actor of the political regime, the right of communities to self-governance and the general process of democratization. Modernization of the institution of local self-government takes place in the creation of appropriate national models, where general rules are adapted to the internal specifics of systemic reforms. The modern stage of the theoretical and applied design of the institute of local self-government is represented by models of the organization of the system of local self-government in European countries.

Among the features of local self-government models in European states, the authors singled out the observance of the principles of subsidiarity (bottom-up state management) and transparency (expanding public participation in the processes of determining the goals and programs of social development). These principles enable the institutional viability of such characteristics of state policy as local (subsidiary) and self-governing (transparent). Also among the identified features are efficiency, service orientation, decentralization, development, implementation and administration of policies, and commitment to consolidation/unification of self-governing units with simultaneous increase in their real powers. The importance of various associations and unions of local self-governments (Denmark, Finland, Lithuania, Sweden, Latvia, Estonia, etc.), whose main task is representation of interests in relations with government structures, is emphasized.

The cases of those countries that are comparable to Ukraine (France, Sweden, Germany) and the study of the experience of the territorial organization of the authorities, which are expedient due to similar processes in Ukraine, are of particular relevance. It is summarized that France and Germany have gone through a rather long way of harmonizing the positions of the political elite, studying and evaluating the capacity of communities, choosing the optimal ratio of distributed powers between the center and regions, and these processes are not exhaustive, because in the last few years new stages of reforms have begun in both countries. In the formation of the system of local self-government, Sweden placed an emphasis on effective control over the implementation of administrative powers on the ground and increasing the role of self-government institutions in the qualitative transformation of the socio-economic sphere (primarily through the activities of the Swedish Association of Local Authorities and Regions). Therefore, the practice of multi-level communication, institutional evolution and enhanced subjectivity of local self-governments can become a guarantee of successful implementation of the reform in Ukraine.

The main trends of modern decentralization processes in Ukraine are substantiated. In order to assess the communities' vision of their own prospects and activity priorities, strategies and plans for the social and economic development of the UTCs were analyzed. The common desire of the communities for economic growth, infrastructure development, improvement of investment potential, and introduction of energy-saving technologies, but without orientation to the support of the central government, has been established. The positive impact of the specifics of the approved strategies on the improvement of institutional memory at the level of regional policy is noted and argued. Another trend is related to the functioning of the institution of local self-government under martial law, which caused a certain pause in the full implementation of their legally established powers by local self-government bodies.

The course and features of the 2020 local elections are analyzed. The democratic nature and corresponding consequences of the 2020 elections can be seen in political communication between the candidate and the voter and the reduction of the distance between them, the restart of the work of party centers, which have turned into important platforms for establishing information and communication links relations of the center and regions, local authorities and the community, a kind of reporting by local party members regarding the activities of the winners of the 2019 elections.

The urgency of expanding the boundaries of perception of the fact of cooperation between communities is emphasized, because they can implement various meaningful interactions, including with foreign institutions, communities, etc. We emphasize the need for the development and deepening of international contacts of communities regarding the attraction of investments and other donor aid, the implementation of joint projects with sister cities, and strengthening the political and legal subjectivity of territorial communities in the context of participation in international relations, in particular cross-border ones. The importance of deepening partnership relations, which since the beginning of the full-scale Russian-Ukrainian war, have been functioning as humanitarian missions to save settlements and Ukrainians affected by Russian aggression both inside the country and abroad (internal and external refugees).

The authors differentiate the challenges of decentralization in the following directions: integration – related to the adaptation of European norms into the institutional component of the functioning of local self-government in Ukraine; orientational – encourage the need for actual, rather than formal, observance of the principle of subsidiarity during the delegation and execution of management powers at the local level; harmonization – is a consequence of the imbalance of the functions and competences obtained by the local self-governments and the personnel potential, experience, and other resources available to them; World-viewing – based on the uncertainty of priorities in the management and development of the economy of communities, associated with the persistent dependence of the UTCs on the center.

The processes of European integration and decentralization of power, united by the subject field of research, are mutually complementary and constitute a priority of the modern state-building stage of Ukraine. At the same time, the realities of the full-scale war of the Russian Federation, which began on February 24, 2022, led to a reassessment of the content of the capacity of territorial communities and the European integration potential of the state, mobilized all possible resources, including diplomatic ones, in order to strengthen resistance to the aggressor and protect the civilians.

Bibliography

Association Agreement between the European Union and its Member States, of the one part, and Ukraine, of the other part. *Official Journal of the European Union*, L 161, 29 May 2014 https://eur-lex.europa.eu/legal-content/EN/TXT/?uri=OJ:L:2014:161:TOC

Bonnal J. *A History of Decentralization*. Columbia University. 2013. URL: http://www.ciesin.org/decentralization/English/General/history_fao.html

Brezovnik B., I.. Hoffman and Ja Kostrubiec. *Local Self-Government in Europe*. Institute for Local Self-Government Maribor, Slovenia, 2021. 445 p.

Burke W. and M. Teller. *A Guide to Owning Transparency. How Federal Agencies Can Implement and Benefit from Transparency*. Washington: Open Forum Foundation, 2009. 88 p. URL: https://www.academia.edu/7758087/A_Guide_To_Owning_Transparency_How_Federal_Agencies_can_Implement_and_Benefit_from_Transparency

Haydanka Y. Authoritarization or Democratization: Directions of Electoral Processes in Present-day Slovakia – *Journal of Comparative Politics* 14(2):4–16, 2021.

Haydanka Y. and M. Martinkovic. *Decentralization and Electoral Processes. Political Fragmentation of the Czech Republic*. Trnava: Akademia, 2022. 118 p.

Haydanka Yevheniy and Marcel Martinkovič. *Socio-Political Fragmentation and Peculiarities of Transboundary Cooperation of the Highest Self-government Body: (on the Example of the Trnava Region of the Slovak Republic)* In: Hileya. – ISSN 2076-1554. – č. 11 (2017), s. 483–487.

Charrad M. Central and Local Patrimonialism: State-Building in Kin-Based Societies. *The Annals of the American Academy of Political and Social Science*. 2011. № 636, P. 49–68.

Colletta C. L'evoluzione storico-legislativa delle autonomie locali: gli Enti Locali nell'ordinamento italiano. *Diritto.it*. 2021. URL: https://www.diritto.it/levoluzione-storico-legislativa-delle-autonomie-locali-gli-enti-locali-nellordinamento-italiano/

Decentralizácia verejnej správy 2003–2006. April 2003. URL: https://www.komunal.eu/images/pdf/Projekt_decentralizacie_2003_2006.pdf

Decentralization Index. *European Committee of the Regions*. 2022. URL: https://portal.cor.europa.eu/divisionpowers/Pages/Decentralization-Index

Declaration of the Assembly of European regions on regionalism in Europe (Basel, 4.12.1996). *Assembly of European Regions: Web-Site*. URL: www.aer.eu/fileadmin/user_upload/PressComm/Publications/DeclarationRegionalism/.dam/l10n/ua/DR_UKRAINE[1].pdf

Déconcentration et décentralisation: définition et différences. *Pamplemousse Magazine*. 2023. URL: https://www.pamplemousse-magazine.co/post/deconcentration-decentralisation-definition-differences

Denmark's Constitution of 1953. *Constituteproject.org*. URL: https://www.constituteproject.org/constitution/Denmark_1953.pdf?lang=en

Discours de M. Gaston Defferre, ministre de l'intérieur et de la décentralisation, au congrès des présidents des conseils généraux, sur le projet de loi relatif à la répartition des compétences, Lyon le 23 septembre 1982. *Vie-publique.fr.* URL: https://www.vie-publique.fr/discours/256670-gaston-defferre-23091982-repartition-des-competences

EmeseP. Models of Legal Supervision over Local SelfGovernments in Continental Europe (Excluding France). *Pécs Journal of International and European Law.* 2018. № 2. P. 6–20.

Emiatt sem kell szégyenkeznie Magyarországnak. *Rigo Kiadója A Mediaworks Hungary.* 2018. URL: https://www.origo.hu/itthon/20180123-nepszavazasok-es-helyi-referendumok-magyarorszagon.html

European Charter of Local Self-Government (Strasbourg, 15.10.1985). *Council of Europe Portal.* URL: https://rm.coe.int/european-charter-of-local-self-government-gbr-a6/16808d7b2d Facondini L. Gliordinamentidelleautonomielocali – iComuni, leProvinceeleCittà metropolitane. *Diritto.it.* 2021. URL: https://www.diritto.it/gli-ordinamenti-delle-autonomie-locali-i-comuni-le-province-e-le-citta-metropolitane/

Finland – Unitary State Organized on a Decentralized Basis. *European Committee of the Regions.* 2022. URL: https://portal.cor.europa.eu/divisionpowers/Pages/Finland.aspx

Finland's Constitution of 1999 (with Amendments through 2011). *Constituteproject.org.* URL: https://www.constituteproject.org/constitution/Finland

France's Constitution of 1958 (with Amendments through 2008). *Constituteproject.org.* URL: https://www.constituteproject.org/constitution/France

Gierke O. von. *Das deutsche Genossenschaftsrecht.* Berlin: Weidmann, 1868.

Gneist R. Selfgovernment, *Communalverfassung und Verwaltungsgerichte in England. 3-te Aufl.* Berlin: Verlag von Julius Springer, 1871. 885 s.

Grundgesetz für die Bundesrepublik Deutschland hat am 23. Mai 1949. URL: http://www.gesetze-im-internet.de/bundesrecht/gg/gesamt.pdf

Kaspar M. *Entwicklungen, Unterschiede und Gemeinsamkeiten der deutschen Kommunalverfassungen.* Universität Konstanz, 2006. URL: https://d-nb.info/1081295880/34

Kaufman H. Administrative Decentralization and Political Power. *Public Administration Review.* 1969. № 29. P. 3–15.

Kettl Donald F. The Global Revolution in Public Management: Driving Themes, Missing Links. *Journal of Policy Analysis and Management.* 1997 John Wiley & Sons, Ltd., vol. 16(3),. p. 446–462.

Koncepce Klientsky orientovaná veřejná správa 2030. Ministerstvo vnitra České republiky. 2020. URL: https://www.mvcr.cz/clanek/koncepce-klientsky-orientovana-verejna-sprava-2030.aspx

La loi Defferre sur la décentralisation est promulguée. *Services de la Première ministre.* 2019. URL: https://www.gouvernement.fr/partage/10896-2-mars-1982-la-loi-defferre-sur-la-decentralisation-est-promulguee

La révision constitutionnelle relative à l'organisation décentralisée de la République, acte II de la décentralisation. *Vie-publique.fr.* 2019. URL: https://www.vie-publique.fr/eclairage/38440-lacte-ii-de-la-decentralisation-la-revision-constitutionnelle#1%E2%80%99autonomie-financi%C3%A8re-des-collectivit%C3%A9s-territoriales

Latvijas Republikas Satversme. (Latvijas Satversmes Sapulces 1922. gada 15. februāra kopsēdē pieņemtā). *Latvijas Republikas tiesību akti*. URL: https://likumi.lv/ta/id/57980-latvijas-republikas-satversme

Leverotti F. Leggi del principe, leggi della città nel ducato visconteo-sforzesco. In: Signori, regimi signorili e statuti nel tardo medioevo. *VII Convegno del Comitato italiano per gli studi e le edizioni delle fonti normative*. Pàtron: Bologna, 2003. P. 143–188.

Marchuk Vasyl. *Ukraine's European integration in the Political Dimension of Central and Eastern Europe*. Trnava: Akademia. 2022. 95 p.

Marchuk Vasyl and Vasyl Dudkevych. *European Integration of Ukraine: Political and Security Practices*.Trnava: Akademia, 2022. 144 p.

Marchuk V., Nataliya Marchuk and Olha Yemets. *Decentralization Reform and Prospects for Economic Development in Ukraine: Impact Assessment// Proceedings of the 36th International Business Information Management Association Conference (IBIMA): Sustainable Economic Development and Advancing Education Excellence in the era of Global Pandemic* / Soliman, Khalid S. (ur.). Granada: International Business Information Management Association (IBIMA), 2020. P.12530–12534.

Marchuk V., Yuliia Kobets, Nataliya Marchuk, Mariana Mishchuk and Olena Berezovska-Chmil. Political And Economic Tools to Support Decentralization Reform and Regional Development Policy in Ukraine // *Proceedings of the 37th International Business Information Management Association (IBIMA)*, / Soliman, Khalid S. (ur.). Cordoba, Spain: P. 12034–12039.

Martinkovič M. Coalition Governments and Development of the Party System in Slovakia / Peter Lang GmbH — VEDA, Publishing House International Academic Publishers of the Slovak Academy of Sciences Bratislava —2021 123 p.

Melnychuk V., V. Marchuk, V. Hladiy, N. Holubiak and V. Dudkevych. The Development of a System of Local Self Government in the Countries of the Visegrad Group in the Conditions of Postmodern Society. *Postmodern Openings*. 2021. № 12 (2). P. 233–245.

Melnychuk V., V. Marchuk, I. Novoselshyi, T. Shlemkevych and V. Chorooyskyi. The Appointment of the History Philosophy in Comprehending Modern Civilizational Challenges in a Post-Pandemic Society. *Postmodern Openings*. 2020. № 11 (1/2). P. 74–84.

Melnychuk V., Yu. Nemish and H. Borshch. Decentralization and Its Influence on Local Community Development. *Economics, Finance and Management Review*. 2020. № 4. P. 4–12.

Miestna samospráva bude vedieť reagovať na nové trendy, umožní to operačný program Efektívna verejná správa. *Ministerstvo vnútra SR*. 2018. URL: https://www.minv.sk/?aktuality_zahranicna_pomoc_MV_SR&sprava=miestna-samosprava-bude-vediet-reagovat-na-nove-trendy-umozni-to-operacny-program-efektivna-verejna-sprava

Mill, J. S. *On Liberty by John Stuart Mill*. United Kingdom: Longmans, Green, and Company, 1867.

Mohl R. *Die Geschichte und Literatur der Staatswissenschaften in Monographieen dargestellt.* Taschenbuch: Adamant Media Corporation, 2001. 619 p.

Mookherjee1 D. *Political Decentralization.* Boston University: Department of Economics, 2014. URL: https://www.bu.edu/econ/files/2015/04/Mookher-jee_PolDecentAREDec14v2.pdf

On the application of the principles of subsidiarity and proportionality (Protocol 12008E/PRO/02). *Official Journal of the European Union.* 2008. № 115. P. 206–209.

Opinion on the new Constitution of Hungary. *Adopted by the Venice Commission at its 87th Plenary Session* (Venice, 17–18 June 2011). Venice Commission, 2011. URL: https://www.venice.coe.int/webforms/documents/default.aspx?pdffile=CDL-AD(2011)016-e

Ozmen A. Notes to the Concept of Decentralization. *European Scientific Journal.* 2014. № 10. P. 415–424.

Proudhon P.-J. *The Principle of Federation.* 1863. URL: https://libcom.org/files/P.-J.%20Proudhon%20-%20The%20Principle%20of%20Federation.pdf

Schaeffner W. Geschichte der Rechtsverfassung Frankreichs: Bis auf Hugo Capet (1849). Sauerländer: Nabu Press, 2012. 696 p.

Slavinskaite N. The Fiscal Decentralization Initiative for Central and Eastern Europe. *Global Journal of Business Economics and Management Current Issues.* 2017. № 7(1):69. URL: https://www.researchgate.net/publication/316067928_Fiscal_decentralization_in_Central_and_Eastern_Europe

Stein L. *Handbuch der Verwaltungslehre. 3-te Aufl., I Theil.* Stuttgart: Verlag der J. G. Coltaschen Buchhandlung, 1888. 565 s.

Subnational Governments in OECD Countries. URL: http://www.oecd.org/regional/Subnational-governments-in-OECD-Countries-Key-Data-2018.pdf

Subsidiarity. Glossary of Summaries. *EUR-Lex. AccesstoEuropeanUnionlaw.* URL: https://eur-lex.europa.eu/summary/glossary/subsidiarity.html

The Constitution of the Republic of Poland (2nd April, 1997). URL: https://www.sejm.gov.pl/prawo/konst/angielski/kon1.htm

Törvény a népszavazás kezdeményezéséről, az európai polgári kezdeményezésről, valamint a népszavazási eljárásról (évi CCXXXVIII). Wolters Kluwer. 2013. URL: https://mkogy.jogtar.hu/jogszabaly?docid=a1300238.TV

Törvény Magyarország helyi önkormányzatairól (évi CLXXXIX). Wolters Kluwer. 2011. URL: https://net.jogtar.hu/jogszabaly?docid=a1100189.tv

Tocqueville, A. d. *Democracy in America.* United Kingdom: University of Chicago Press, 2002.

Treisman D. Political Decentralization and Economic Reform: A Game-Theoretic Analysis. *American Journal of Political Science.* 1999. № 43. P. 488–517.

Ustawa z dnia 15 września 2000 r. o referendum lokalnym. Strona główna

Sejmu Rzeczpospolitej Polskiej. URL: https://sip.lex.pl/akty-prawne/dzu-dziennik-ustaw/referendum-lokalne-16885627

Verbal de L'assemblée Nationale, sur la Constitution des Municipalités: Extrait du Procès (du 14 Décembre 1789). URL: https://legilux.public.lu/eli/etat/leg/dec/1789/12/14/n1/jo

Vietējo pašvaldību referendumu likums (Likums stājas spēkā 2024. gada 1. janvārī.). *Latvijas Republikas tiesību akti*. URL: https://likumi.lv/ta/id/331194-vietejo-pasvaldibu-referendumu-likums

Vinnykova N. Risks of Political Non-decision-making (applications toUkraine). *Politicus*. 2020. № 5. P. 35–43.

Young D. *Local Government in the Nordic and Baltic Countries*: An Overview. SKL International, 2016. URL: http://sklinternational.org.ua/wp-content/uploads/2016/09/SKL20International20HELA20160426.pdf

Yuliani E. Decentralization, Deconcentration and Devolution: What Do They Mean? *Interlaken Workshop on Decentralization (27–30 April 2004, Interlaken, Switzerland)*. URL: https://www.cifor.org/publications/pdf_files/interlaken/Compilation.pdf

Zajíček Ja. Místní samosprávy a manažeři místní samosprávy v sedmnácti evropských zemích. *Veřejná správa*. 2008. № 8. URL: https://www.mvcr.cz/clanek/mistni-samospravy-a-manazeri-mistni-samospravy-v-sedmnacti-evropskych-zemich-i.aspx

Zákon č. 51/2020 Sb., o územně správním členění státu. Ministerstvo vnitra České republiky. 2021. URL: https://storymaps.arcgis.com/stories/27ada7f9e22d4e9290f1aaa5ccb31c96

Абасов Г. огли. Методи дослідження гарантій прав місцевого самоврядування: проблеми конституційно-правової теорії. *Конституційне право та конституційний процес в Україні*. 2012. № 3. С. 96–100.

Агафонова Г. Ірха К., Дудкевич В. Стан реалізації соціально-економічних трансформацій в Україні у контексті політики євроінтеграції. *Вісник Національного технічного університету України «Київський політехнічний інститут». Серія «Політологія. Соціологія. Право»*. 2021. № 4 (52). С. 39–46.

Агафонова Г., Ірха К. Внутрішній і зовнішній виміри співробітництва територіальних громад в Україні. *Вісник Національного технічного університету України «Київський політехнічний інститут». Серія «Політологія. Соціологія. Право»*. 2022. № 4. С. 42–50.

Агафонова Г., Сімонян А. Типологізація громадських рад. *Гілея: науковий вісник. Збірник наукових праць*. 2018. № 137. С. 283–287.

Аналіз громад. *Децентралізація: Офіційний вебпортал.*URL: https://storage.decentralization.gov.ua/uploads/attachment/document/391/%D0%90%D0%BD%D0%B0%D0%BB%D1%96%D0%B7_%D0%B3%D1%80%D0%BE%D0%BC%D0%B0%D0%B4.pdf

Андрейчук І., Конкольняк М. Оцінювання інвестиційної привабливості об'єднаних територіальних громад у гірських регіонах на основі державного регулювання. *Економіка та суспільство.* 2021. № 27. URL: https://economyandsociety. in.ua/index.php/journal/article/view/454/436

Бабаєв В. *Управління великим містом: теоретичні і прикладні аспекти: монографія.* Х.: ХНАМГ, 2010. 307 с.

Баймуратов М. Муніципальне право України: підручник. Київ: Правова єдність, 2009. 716 с.

Батракова Д. *Адміністративно-правове регулювання місцевого самоврядування: порівняльно-правовий аналіз України та Франції.* Дис. на здобуття наук. ст. к.ю.н. Київ: Національна академія внутрішніх справ, 2017. 201 с.

Бевз Т. Роль Центральної виборчої комісії у здійсненні реформи децентралізації в Україні (2015–2019 рр.). *Наукові записки.* 2020. № 1. С. 47–68.

Біла-Тіунова Л., Білоус-Осінь Т., Тодощак О. *Децентралізація публічної влади: навч.-метод. посіб.* Одеса: Фенікс, 2023. 66 с.

Богородецька О. *Співробітництво між містами-побратимами України і Польщі у контексті європейської інтеграції.* Дис. на здобуття наук. ст. к.політ.н. Луцьк: Східноєвропейський національний університет імені Лесі Українки, 2015. 232 с.

Бойко Г., Камінська Н. Еволюція місцевого та регіонального самоврядування в умовах розвитку європейської демократії. *Архіви України.* 2014. № 4–5. С. 73–83.

Бориславська О., Заверуха І. (та ін.). *Децентралізація публічної влади:досвід європейських країн та перспективи України.* Швейцарсько-український проєкт «Підтримка децентралізації в Україні – DESPRO. Київ: ТОВ «Софія», 2012. 128 с.

Бородін Є., Шумляєва І. Інституційно-правове забезпечення функціонування суб'єктів місцевого самоврядування в Україні. *Аспекти публічного управління.* 2021. № 3. С. 13–21.

Бриль М. (у співавт.). *Успішна територіальна громада: будуємо разом.* Харків: Видавничий будинок Фактор, 2018. 128 с.

Буглак Ю. Проблеми розмежування повноважень між органами виконавчої влади і органами місцевого самоврядування в Україні. *Підприємництво, господарство і право.* 2018. № 11. С. 70–75.

Буря К. Політико-правові засади легітимації локальної демократії в умовах політичних трансформацій. Дис. на здобуття наук. ст. д-ра філософії. Дніпро: Дніпровський національний університет імені Олеся Гончара. 2021. 220 с.

В умовах децентралізації одним із наших найважливіших завдань є перезавантаження сприйняття економічної привабливості культури на місцевому рівні, – Євген Нищук. *Урядовий портал.* 2017. URL: https://www.kmu.gov.ua/news/249822776

Вебер М. Образ общества. *Избранное.* Москва: Юрист, 1994. С. 324–325.

Великая хартия вольностей (1215 г.). Конституции и законодательные акты буржуазных государств XVII-XIX вв. Сборник *документов.* Москва: Государственное изд-во юридической литературы, 1957. С. 15–22.

Венеційська комісія оприлюднила висновок щодо законопроєкту про місцевий референдум. *Реанімаційний пакет реформ.* 2022. URL: https://rpr.org.ua/news/venetsiyska-komisiia-opryliudnyla-vysnovok-shchodo-zakonoproiektu-pro-mistsevyy-referendum/

Взаємозв'язок між децентралізацією та європейською інтеграцією: Соціологічне опитування. *Центр «Нова Європа» (Україна); Центр східноєвропейських та міжнародних досліджень (ZOiS, Німеччина).* 2020. URL: http://neweurope.org.ua/wp-content/uploads/2020/02/Decentralization_ukr_web-2.pdf

Виборчий кодекс України від 19.12.2019 р. *Верховна Рада України: Офіційний вебпортал. URL:* https://zakon.rada.gov.ua/laws/show/396-20#Text

Відкрите звернення голів районних рад України стосовно проблемних питань діяльності районних рад до Президента України В. Зеленського. 2021. URL: http://uaror.org.ua/wp-content/uploads/

Вінникова Н. Парадокси політичних рішень в епоху пост демократії: монографія. Харків: ХНУ імені В. Н. Каразіна, 2019. 424 с.

Вінникова Н. Проблема легітимації політичних рішень у контексті деетатизації політичного урядування. *Політикус.* 2019. № 1. С. 29–35.

Гижко А. Світові практики впровадження децентралізації та їх досвід для України. *Політичне життя.* 2020. № 1. С. 22–29.

Гирке О. фон. Германское общественное право. Санкт-Петербург, 1900. 658 с.

Гладій В. Місцеве самоврядування як ресурс політики євроінтеграції: досвід Вишеградської групи та перспективи України. Дис. на здобуття наук. ст. к.політ.н.. Івано-Франківськ: ПНУ ім. В. Стефаника, 2015. 238 с.

Гоголь Т., Мельничук Л. Трансформація територіальних громад в умовах децентралізації в Україні. *Право та державне управління.* 2022. № 1. С. 216–225.

Горбатюк М. Реформа децентралізації в Україні: проблеми здійснення в умовах суспільної кризи. *Політичні дослідження.* 2021. № 1. С. 22–40.

Грицяк І. Державне управління в Україні: централізація і децентралізація. Київ: Вид-во УАДУ, 1997. 487 с.

Гробова В. П. *Система місцевого самоврядування в Україні: проблеми теорії і практики.* Дис. на здобуття наук. ст. д.ю.н. за спеціальністю 12.00.02 – конституційне право. Харків, 2013. 415 с.

Громади, НЕ МОВЧІТЬ! У вас сотні міст-побратимів. Зверніться до них за підтримкою. *Децентралізація:* Офіційний вебпортал. 2022. URL: https://decentralization.gov.ua/news/14626

Громадська думка населення щодо реформи децентралізації та її результатів (серпень 2020 р.). *Фонд «Демократичні ініціативи» ім. Ілька Кучеріва.* URL: https://dif.org.ua/article/gromadska-dumka-naselennya-shchodo-reformi-detsentralizatsii-ta-ii-rezultativ

Гронский П. Децентрализация и самоуправление. Москва: Т-во скоропеч. А. А. Левенсон, 1917. 40 с.

Гурін Д. Про новий законопроект «Про місцеве самоврядування в Україні». 2021. *Децентралізація:* Офіційний вебпортал. 2020. URL: https://decentralization.gov.ua/news/13337

Дацишин М. Як відновити місцеве самоврядування від наслідків війни? *Українська правда.* 2022. URL: https://www.pravda.com.ua/columns/2022/08/5/7362004/

Два ракурси. Місцеві вибори в регіональному й національному вимірах. *Тиждень.* URL: https://tyzhden.ua/Politics/243181

Демиденко Г. Історія вчень про право і державу: хрестоматія. Харків: Легас, 2002. 922 с.

Дерев'янко С. Безпековий вимір народовладдя в умовах гібридної війни. *Держава і право*. 2020. № 87. С. 308–318.

Дерев'янко С. Інститут місцевого референдуму в Україні: доцільність та перспективи оновлення його конституційної моделі. *Прикарпатський вісник НТШ. Серія «Думка»*. 2018. № 5 (49). С. 85–96.

Державна стратегія регіонального розвитку на 2021–2027 рр. Законодавство України. URL: https://zakon.rada.gov.ua/laws/show/695-2020-%D0%BF#Text

Децентралізація влади: порядок денний на середньострокову перспективу. *Національний інститут стратегічних досліджень*. URL: https://niss.gov.ua/sites/default/files/2019

Децентралізація: Офіційний портал. URL: https://decentralization.gov.ua/newgromada

Для урбаністів Ірпінь – це мрія: Японський архітектор Мацура погодився розробити план відбудови міста. *Рубрика*. 2022. URL: https://rubryka.com/2022/06/12/dlya-urbanistiv-irpin-tse-mriya-yaponskyj-arhitektor-matsura-pogodyvsya-rozrobyty-plan-vidbudovy-mista/

Додатковий протокол до Європейської хартії місцевого самоврядування про право участі у справах місцевого органу влади. *Законодавство України*. URL: http://zakon5.rada.gov.ua/laws/show/994_946

Драгоманов М. «Переднє слово до громади» про державну організацію. Київ: Дакор, 2008. 370 с.

Дяконенко О. Розвиток сільських поселень в умовах адміністративно-територіальної реформи. *Матеріали Міжнародної науково-практичної конференції «Адміністративно-територіальні vs економічно-просторові кордони регіонів»*. 2020. URL: https://ir.kneu.edu.ua/bitstream/handle/2010/33457/atepkr_20_78.pdf?sequence=1&isAllowed=y

Еллинек Г. Общее учение о государстве. Санкт-Петербург: Юрид. центр Пресс, 2004. 752 с.

Енциклопедія сучасної України. URL: https://esu.com.ua/article-17370

Європарламент назвав реформу децентралізації найуспішнішою в Україні – Чернишов. *Укрінформ*. 2021. URL: https://www.ukrinform.ua/rubric-polytics/3222717-evroparlament-nazvav-reformu-decentralizacii-najuspisnisou-v-ukraini-cernisov.html

Європарламент: Угорщину більше не можна розглядати як демократію. *Українська правда*. 2022. URL: https://www.pravda.com.ua/news/2022/09/15/7367617/

Європейська хартія місцевого самоврядування (м. Страсбург, 15 жовтня 1985 року): офіційний переклад.*Законодавство України*. URL: https://zakon.rada.gov.ua/laws/show/994_036#Text

Європейські міста-побратими допомагають українським громадам. *Асоціація міст України*: Офіційний вебсайт. 2022. URL: https://auc.org.ua/novyna/yevropeyski-mista-pobratymy-dopomagayut-ukrayinskym-gromadam

Єсімов С., Бондаренко В. Транспарентність як принцип діяльності органів публічного управління в умовах використання інформаційних технологій. *Соціально-правові студії*. 2018. № 1. С. 42–49.

Жаліло Я. Децентралізація і формування політики регіонального розвитку в Україні.Київ: НІСД, 2020. 153 с.

Жук П., Сірик З. Інвестиційний потенціал територіальних громад: суть поняття та питання управління. *Регіональна економіка*. 2017. № 2. С. 16–22.

З відновленням Ірпеня допоможуть країни західних Балкан та італійські компанії. *Рубрика*. 2022. URL: https://rubryka.com/2022/06/18/z-vidnovlennyam-irpenya-dopomozhut-krayiny-zahidnyh-balkan-ta-italijski-kompaniyi/

Загуменна Ю., Лазарєв В. Становлення та розвиток органів місцевого самоврядування в Україні (1991–2019 роки). *Право і безпека*. 2020. № 2 (77). С. 106–117.

Загурська-Антонюк В. Сучасні тенденції децентралізації державної влади та їх реалізація в Україні. *Державне управління: вдосконалення та розвиток*. 2019. № 2. URL: http://www.dy.nayka.com.ua/pdf/2_2019/26.pdf

делегація взяла участь у відзначенні 5-річчя діяльності ЄОТС ТИСА. *Закарпатська обласна рада*: Офіційний вебсайт. 2021. URL: https://zakarpat-rada.gov.ua/zakarpatska-delehatsiia-vziala-uchast-u-vidznachenni-5-richchia-diialnosti-yeots-tysa/

Закарпаття має скористатися перевагами децентралізації і ефективно використати державну та міжнародну допомогу, – В'ячеслав Негода. *Міністерство розвитку громад та територій України*: Офіційний вебсайт. 2016. URL: https://www.minregion.gov.ua/press/news/zakarpattya-maye-skoristatisya-perevagami-detsentralizatsiyi-i-efektivno-vikoristati-derzhavnu-ta-mizhnarodnu-dopomogu-v-yacheslav-negoda/

Закон України «Про внесення змін до деяких законів України щодо функціонування державної служби та місцевого самоврядування у період дії воєнного стану» від 12.05.2022 р. *Верховна Рада України*: Офіційний вебпортал. URL: https://zakon.rada.gov.ua/laws/show/2259-IX#Text

Закон України «Про внесення змін до деяких законодавчих актів України щодо спрощення залучення інвестицій та запровадження нових фінансових інструментів» від 19.06.2020 р. *Верховна Рада України*: Офіційний вебсайт. URL: https://zakon.rada.gov.ua/laws/show/738-20#Text

Закон України «Про громадські об'єднання» від 22.03.2012 р. *Законодавство України*. URL: https://zakon.rada.gov.ua/laws/show/4572-17#Text

Закон України «Про добровільне об'єднання територіальних громад» від 05.02.2015 р. *Верховна Рада України*: Офіційний вебпортал. URL: https://zakon.rada.gov.ua/laws/show/157-19#Text

Закон України «Про засади державної регіональної політики» від 5.02.2015 р. *Верховна Рада України*: Офіційний вебпортал. URL: https://zakon.rada.gov.ua/laws/show/156-19#Text

Закон України «Про захист іноземних інвестицій на Україні» від 10.09.1991 р. *Верховна Рада України*: Офіційний вебсайт. URL: https://zakon.rada.gov.ua/laws/show/1540%D0%B0-12#Text

Закон України «Про інвестиційну діяльність» від 18.09.1991 р. *Верховна Рада України*: Офіційний вебсайт. URL: https://zakon.rada.gov.ua/laws/show/1560-12#Text

Закон України «Про місцеве самоврядування в Україні» від 21.05.1997 р. (зі змінами). *Законодавство України*. URL: https://zakon.rada.gov.ua/laws/show/280/97-%D0%B2%D1%80#Text

Закон України «Про органи самоорганізації населення» від 11.07.2001 р. *Законодавство України*.URL: https://zakon.rada.gov.ua/laws/show/2625-14#Text

Закон України «Про основи національного спротиву» від 16.07.2021 р. *Верховна Рада України*: Офіційний вебсайт. URL: https://zakon.rada.gov.ua/laws/show/1702-20#Text

Закон України «Про правовий режим воєнного стану» від 12.05.2015 р. (зі змінами). *Верховна Рада України:* Офіційний вебпортал. URL: https://zakon.rada.gov.ua/laws/show/389-19#Text

Закон України «Про ратифікацію Європейської Хартії місцевого самоврядування» від 15.07.1997 р.*Верховна Рада України*: Офіційний вебпортал. URL: https://zakon.rada.gov.ua/laws/show/452/97-%D0%B2%D1%80#Text

Закон України «Про службу в органах місцевого самоврядування» від 07.06.2001 р. (зі змінами). *Верховна Рада України*: Офіційний вебпортал. URL:https://zakon.rada.gov.ua/laws/show/2493-14#Text

Закон України «Про співробітництво територіальних громад» від 17.06.2014 р. *Верховна Рада України*: Офіційний вебсайт. URL: https://zakon.rada.gov.ua/laws/show/1508-18#Text

Закон України «Про транскордонне співробітництво» від 24.06.2004 р. *Верховна Рада України*: Офіційний вебсайт. URL: https://zakon.rada.gov.ua/laws/show/1861-15#Text

Закон України «Про участь громадян в охороні громадського порядку і державного кордону» від 22.06.2000 р.*Законодавство України*. URL: https://zakon.rada.gov.ua/laws/show/1835-14#Text

Закон України «Про Цілі сталого розвитку України на період до 2030 року» від 30.09.2019 р.*Законодавство України*. URL: https://zakon.rada.gov.ua/laws/show/722/2019#Text

Законодавство про децентралізацію.*Децентралізація:* Офіційний вебпортал. URL: https://decentralization.gov.ua/legislations?year=&legislation_ type=&legislation_ state=&legislation_topic=&legislation_name=&legislation_number=

Законопроєкт про місцевий референдум: перспективи ухвалення та оцінка Венеційської комісії. *Укрінформ*. 2022. URL: https://www.ukrinform.ua/rubric-presshall/3400793-zakonoproekt-pro-miscevij-referendum-perspektivi-uhvalenna-ta-ocinka-venecijskoi-komisii.html

Інвестиційне законодавство: стан, проблеми, перспективи: Роз'яснення Міністерства юстиції України від 8.05.2012 р. *Верховна Рада України*: Офіційний вебсайт. URL: https://zakon.rada.gov.ua/laws/show/n0015323-12#Text

Камінська Н. Місцеве самоврядування: теоретико-історичний і порівняльно-правовий аналіз. Київ: КНТ, 2010. 232 с.

Кармазіна М. Політичний регіон: підстави формування та функціонування. *Наукові записки*. 2018. № 1(81). С. 4–23.

Кейс-стаді «Впровадження інвестиційних інструментів на регіональному та муніципальному рівнях». *Проєкт міжнародної технічної допомоги «Партнерство для розвитку міст»*. 2020. URL: https://decentralization.gov.ua/uploads/library/file/609/Case_Study_PLEDDG_Investments-web.pdf

Кириленко О. Нові райони України: 15 відповідей на поширені запитання. *Українська правда*. 27 липня 2020 р. URL: https://www.pravda.com.ua/articles/2020/07/27/7260764/

Климончук В. Загальноєвропейські політичні цінності та перспективи їх реалізації в сучасній Україні. *Вісник Прикарпатського університету*. 2013. № 6–7. С. 38–42.

Климончук В., Арделі О. Демократичні трансформації у посткомуністичних країнах Центрально-Східної Європи: інстутиційний вимір. *Вісник Прикарпатського університету. Серія «Політологія»*. 2019. № 13. С. 302–309.

Климончук В., Масик Ю. Особливості перетворення політичних систем Балтійських країн у складі ЄС. *Вісник Прикарпатського університету. Серія «Політологія»*. 2020. № 14. С. 250–257.

Кобець Ю. Еволюція політичної системи сучасної України: трансформаційні виклики та особливості реформування після 2014 року. *Прикарпатський вісник НТШ. Серія «Думка»*. 2017. № 5–6 (41–42). С. 51–58.

Кобець Ю. Особливості регіональної політики сучасної Греції крізь призму політики Європейського Союзу. *Вісник Прикарпатського університету. Серія «Політологія»*. 2016. №10. С. 113–117.

Кобець Ю., Мадрига Т. ЯКІСТЬ політичної еліти України в контексті демократичних перетворень. *Прикарпатський вісник НТШ. Серія «Думка»*. 2019. № 4 (56). С. 70–80.

Кобилецький М. Магдебурзьке право в Україні. *Wrocławsko-Lwowskie Zeszyty Prawnicze*. 2019. № 10. С. 9–21.

Ковбасюк Ю., Орлатий М. (за заг. ред.). *Адміністративно-територіальний устрій країн Європейського Союзу: навч. посіб.* К.: НАДУ, 2015. 628 с.

Колишко Р. Децентралізація публічної влади: історія та сучасні тенденції розвитку. *Вісник КНУ*. 2003. № 27. С. 198–204.

Комарницький В. Роль партійного чинника в реалізації електоральних стратегій (на прикладі місцевих виборів 2020 року). *Вісник Національного технічного університету України «Київський політехнічний інститут». Серія «Політологія. Соціологія. Право»*. 2020. № 1 (45). С. 19–24. URL: http://visnyk-psp.kpi.ua/article/view/226468/226072

Комплексна програма розвитку міжнародного співробітництва, європейської інтеграції та залучення міжнародної технічної допомоги на 2011–2013 роки. *Офіційний сайт Івано-Франківської міської ради*. URL: https://www.mvk.if.ua/uploads/files/ek_program_121110.pdf

Кондратьєва А. Організація управління розвитком територій під час військових дій в Україні. *Громадський простір*. 2022. URL: https://www.prostir.ua/?library=orhanizatsiya-upravlinnya-rozvytkom-terytorij-pid-chas-vijskovyh-dij-v-ukrajini

Конституція Італійської Республіки (з передмовою Володимира Шаповала). Київ: Москаленко О. М., 2018. 62 с.

Конституція України (від 28.06.1996 р. зі змінами). *Президент України*: Офіційне інтернет-представництво. URL: https://www.president.gov.ua/ua/documents/constitution/konstituciya-ukrayini-rozdil-xi Конфлікт Прилуцької райради та Ладанської громади. *Громади Чернігівщини*. 2021. URL: https://otg.cn.ua/2021/04/02/news-gromady/ladanska/konflikt-prylutskoyi-rajrady-ta-ladanskoyi-gromady/

Концепція реформування місцевого самоврядування та територіальної організації влади в Україні від 01.04.2014 р. *Законодавство України*. URL: https://zakon.rada.gov.ua/laws/show/333-2014-%D1%80#Text

Концепція розвитку сільських територій від 23.09.2015 р. *Верховна Рада України:* Офіційний вебсайт. URL: https://zakon.rada.gov.ua/laws/show/995-2015-%D1%80#Text

Концепція стимулювання розвитку підприємництва на сільських територіях до 2030 року. *Міністерство аграрної політики та продовольства України: Офіційний вебсайт.* 2021. URL: https://minagro.gov.ua/npa/pro-shvalennya-koncepciyi-stimulyuvannya-rozvitku-pidpriyemnictva-na-silskih-teritoriyah-do-2030-roku

Концепція удосконалення законодавства про місцеві вибори у зв'язку з реформуванням місцевого самоврядування та адміністративно-територіального устрою. *Децентралізація*: Офіційний вебпортал.URL: https://decentralization.gov.ua/uploads/attachment/document/464/.pdf

Корицька В. Характеристика та сутність основних моделей місцевого самоврядування: на прикладах розвинених країн світу. *Сучасна українська політика. Політики і політологи про неї.* 2008. № 13. С. 224–237.

Корчинська О. Управління соціально-економічним розвитком об'єднаних територіальних громад. *Вісник Національного університету «Львівська політехніка».* 2019. № 7. С. 81–88.

Костицький В. Місцеве самоврядування як окрема гілка публічної влади. *Вісник АПСВТ.* 2018. № 1. С. 48–50.

Красівський О., Янішевський М. Еволюція системи місцевого самоврядування у Німеччині (на прикладі землі Бранденбург): історико-управлінський аспект. *Аспекти публічного управління.* 2016. № 6–7. С. 85–94.

Критерії ефективних організаційних структур виконавчих органів місцевого самоврядування України: аналітична записка. *Децентралізація:* Офіційний вебпортал. 2019. URL: https://decentralization.gov.ua/uploads/library/file/476/new_KO.pdf

Курбатов Г. Город и государство в Византии в эпоху перехода от античности к феодализму. Ленинград: Изд-во Ленинград. ун-та, 1982. 245 с.

Лелеченко А., Васильєва О., Куйбіда В. Місцеве самоврядування в умовах децентралізації повноважень: навч. посіб. Київ, 2017. 110 с.

Лондар Л. Напрями реалізації політики децентралізації в умовах розширення прав місцевих органів влади і забезпечення їх фінансової та бюджетної самостійності: аналітична записка. *Національний інститут стратегічних досліджень.* 2016. URL: https://niss.gov.ua/doslidzhennya/ekonomika/napryami-realizacii-politiki-decentralizacii-v-umovakh-rozshirennya-prav

Майно громад: чому і як в Мінрегіоні планують змінити норми законодавства, що регулюють питання комунальної власності. *Децентралізація:* Офіційний веб-портал. 2021. URL: https://decentralization.gov.ua/news/14080

Макаренко Л., Сергов С. Теоретичні засади дослідження процесів становлення системи місцевої влади в Україні. *Історико-політичні студії.* 2018. № 2 (10). С. 64–75.

Макаруха З. Засадничі принципи заснування та розвитку простору свободи, безпеки та юстиції в рамках ЄС. *Актуальні проблеми міжнародних відносин.* 2009. № 84. С. 180–191.

Маланчук О. Бюджетна децентралізація: реальний вплив на фінансове забезпечення та розподіл видатків територіальних громад. *Громадський простір.* 2017. URL: https://www.prostir.ua/?news=byudzhetna-detsentralizatsiya-realnyj-vplyv-na-finansove-zabezpechennya-ta-rozpodil-vydatkiv-terytorialnyh-hromad

Малиновський В. Словник термінів і понять з державного управління. Київ: Центр сприяння інституц. розв. держ. служби, 2005. 234 с.

Мануілова К. Форми адміністративної децентралізації влади: сутність, класифікації, переваги та недоліки. *Публічне управління та адміністрування в Україні.* 2018. № 3. С. 13–16.

Маркетингова стратегія Гірської об'єднаної територіальної громади. 2021. URL: https://rada.info/upload/users_files/33976099/164926f138a43d8471bccad2148ca0e1.pdf

Мартинов А. Європейська інтеграція. *Енциклопедія історії України.* Київ: Наукова думка, 2005. Т. 3. 672 с.

Марчук В. Вибори і виборчі системи. Івано-Франківськ: ЛІК. 2019. 79 с.

Марчук В. Громадянська активність та ефективне управління як основи соціального партнерства. *Побудова миру та справедливості на перехресті цивілізацій. Місія України.* Київ, 2016. С. 105–131.

Марчук В., Гладій В. Моделі місцевого самоврядування: європейський досвід і реалії України. *Вісник Прикарпатського університету. Серія «Політологія».* 2020. № 14. С. 215–223.

Марчук В., Гладій В. Моделі місцевого самоврядування: європейський досвід і реалії України. Вісник Прикарпатського університету. Серія «Політологія». 2020. № 14. С. 215–223

Н.Марчук. Використання інструментів PR в органах місцевого самоврядування на прикладі Івано-Франківської області.// Вісник Прикарпатського університету. Політологія. Випуск 14, 2020. с.55–59

Матвєєва Л. Теорія та практика побудови і розвитку демократичної, соціальної, правової держави в Україні у контексті євроінтеграції: колективна монографія. Одеса: РВВ ОДУВС, 2021. 290 с.

Маурер Г. Введение в историю общинного, подворного, сельского и городского устройства и общественной власти. Москва: К. Т. Солдатенков, 1880. 358 с.

Мельник Я. Іноземні моделі та досвід децентралізації публічного управління. *Вчені записки ТНУ імені В.І. Вернадського. Серія «Державне управління».* 2020. Том 31 (70) № 3. С. 155–163.

Мельничук В. Аспекти конструювання національної моделі територіальної органі- зації влади в Україні. *Матеріали всеукраїнської науково-практичної конференції з міжнародною участю «Майбутній науковець – 2021» (м. Сєвєродонецьк, 3 грудня 2021 р.).* Сєвєродонецьк: Східноукр. нац. ун-т ім. В. Даля, 2021. С. 262–264.

Мельничук В. Євроінтеграційний чинник реформування місцевого самовря- дування в Україні. *Перспективи розвитку наукових досліджень у контексті глобалізаційних змін: освіта, політика, економіка, міжкультурна комунікація: Матеріали V міжнар. наук.-практ. конф. (м. Сєвєродонецьк, 8 червня 2021 р.).* Сєвєродонецьк: Вид-во СНУ ім. В. Даля, 2021. С. 101–105.

Мельничук В. Зв'язок системи місцевого самоврядування та реалізації курсу європейської інтеграції України. *Пріоритетні напрями наукових досліджень: філософський, політологічний та культурологічний аспекти: Матеріали між- народної науково-практичної конференції (м. Київ, 8–9 жовтня 2021 р.).* Київ: Таврійський національний університет імені В. І. Вернадського, 2021. С. 46–50.

Мельничук В. Імплементація принципів європейської хартії місцевого самовря- дування в контексті децентралізації влади. *Вісник Прикарпатського університе- ту. Серія «Політологія».* 2019. № 13. С. 111–118.

Мельничук В. Історія децентралізаційних процесів і Україна. *Дослідження інновацій та перспективи розвитку науки і техніки у XXI столітті: Матері- али Міжнародної науково-практичної конференції (м. Рівне, 25–26 листопада 2021 р.).* Рівне: Видавничий дім «Гельветика», 2021. Ч. 4. С. 19–22.

Мельничук В. Місцеве самоврядування та територіальна організація влади на субрегіональному рівні: пошуки компромісу. *Вісник Прикарпатського універси- тету. Серія «Політологія».* 2020. № 14. С. 303–314.

Мельничук В. Місцеві вибори – 2020 в умовах децентралізації влади: виклики для місцевого самоврядування. *Вісник Прикарпатського університету. Серія «Політологія».* 2020. № 14. С. 59–64.

Мельничук В. Російсько-українська війна як чинник впливу на зміст регіональ- ного виміру міжнародного співробітництва. *Матеріали VII Міжнародної на- уково-практичної конференції «Формат розвитку відносин України та країн Центральної Європи у контексті російсько-української війни» (м. Ужгород, 23 вересня 2022 р.).* Ужгород: Вид-во УжНУ, 2022. С. 74–78.

Мельничук В. Специфіка конструювання моделей місцевого самоврядування в країнах Європейського Союзу. *Вісник Львівського університету. Серія «Філо- софсько-політологічні студії».* 2022. № 42. С. 278–285.

Мельничук В. Феномен регіональної самоврядності. *Перспективи розвитку нау- кових досліджень у контексті глобалізаційних змін: освіта, політика, економіка, міжкультурна комунікація: матеріалиV Міжнародної науково-практичної кон- ференції (м. Кам'янець-Подільський, 20 травня 2022 р.).* Сєвєродонецьк: Вид-во СНУ ім. В. Даля, 2022. С. 108–111.

Мельничук В. Чинники формування регіональної самоврядності в Україні. *По- літикус.* 2021. № 6. С. 37–43.

Мельничук В., Марчук В. Стан інтеграції європейського досвіду у функціону- вання системи місцевого самоврядування України. *Регіональні студії.* 2022. № 31. С. 117–124.

Методика формування спроможних територіальних громад від 24.01.2020 р. *Верховна Рада України*: Офіційний вебпортал. URL: https://zakon.rada.gov.ua/laws/show/214-2015-%D0%BF#Text

Методичні рекомендації щодо критеріїв формування адміністративно-територіальних одиниць субрегіонального (районного) рівня. Київ, 2019. URL: https://www.minregion.gov.ua/wp-content/uploads/2019/08/Metod.recom_.rayon_.pdf

Методичні рекомендації щодо розроблення Статуту територіальної громади. Київ, 2019. URL: https://decentralization.gov.ua/uploads/library/file/391/Recommend.pdf

Митяй О., Світовий О. Публічне управління територіальною спільнотою в Україні. *Державне управління: удосконалення та розвиток*. 2016. URL: http://www.dy.nayka.com.ua/pdf/4_2018/38.pdf

Міжнародний марафон місцевого самоврядування об'єднав більше 1000 муніципалітетів з 35 країн. Діалог продовжать. *Децентралізація*: Офіційний вебпортал. 2022. URL: https://decentralization.gov.ua/news/14792

Міль Дж. С. Про свободу. Київ: Основи, 2001. 366 с.

Мільбрадт Ґ. Україна повинна думати на перспективу. *Укрінформ*. 2019. URL: https://www.ukrinform.ua/rubric-regions/2647503-georg-milbradt-specialnij-predstavnik-uradu-nimeccini.html

Місцевий економічний розвиток у територіальних громадах: корисні поради та кращі практики. *Децентралізація*: Офіційний вебпортал. 2021. URL: https://decentralization.gov.ua/uploads/library/file/717/MER_2021_WEB.pdf

Місцеві вибори восени 2020 і реформа децентралізації: куди обирати і як організовувати. *Опора*. URL: https://www.oporaua.org/news/samovriaduvannia/19921-mistsevi-vibori-voseni2020-i-reforma-detsentralizatsiyi-kudi-obirati-i-iak-organizovuvati

Місцеві вибори за новими правилами: чому знову треба змінювати виборче законодавство і що пропонують експерти. *Децентралізація*: Офіційний вебпортал. URL: https://decentralization.gov.ua/news/11728

Місцеві вибори-2020: проблемні питання підготовки. URL: http://nbuviap.gov.ua/index.php?option=com_content&view=article&id=4906:mistsevivibori-2020-problemni-pitannya-pidgotovki-2&catid=64&Itemid=376

Моніторинг місцевих виборів 2020: підсумки. *Соціологічна група «Рейтинг»*. 2020. URL: https://ratinggroup.ua/research/ukraine/monitoring_mestnyh_vyborov_2020_itogi.html

Монолатій І. Міжгрупові інтеракції в етнополітичному дискурсі: проблеми теорії та методології. Івано-Франківськ: Лілея-НВ, 2011. 191 с.

Монолатій І. Сила ЗУНР: вибрані питання потенціалу, безпеки і дипломатії держави. Івано-Франківськ: Лілея-НВ, 2020. 87 с.

Монолатій І., Великочий В., Плекан Ю. «Були трактовані наскрізь гуманно…». Косачівський табір для інтерованих осіб в контексті українсько-польських взаємин у Галичині (1918–1919 рр.): колективна монографія. Івано-Франківськ: Видавець Кушнір Г. М., 2019. 182 с.

Мошак О. Правовий зміст принципу субсидіарності в умовах євроінтеграції України. *Lex Portus*. 2017. № 3 (5). С. 35–48.

Муніципальна реформа в контексті євроінтеграції України: позиція влади, науковців, профспілок та громадськості. *Тези доповідей Третьої щорічної всеукраїнської науково-практичної конференції* (м. Київ, 06 грудня 2019 р.). Київ: ТОВ «ВІ ЕН ЕЙ ПРЕС», 2019. 228 с.

Населення України. *Державна служба статистики*: Офіційний вебресурс. URL: https://ukrstat.gov.ua/operativ/operativ2007/ds/nas_rik/nas_u/nas_rik_u.html

Неусыхин А. Социологическое исследование М. Вебера о городе. Москва: Юрист, 1994. С. 640–678.

Нечай Ф. Рим и италики. Москва: Рипол Классик, 2013. 202 с.

Новак А. Делегування повноважень у механізмі децентралізації державної влади в Україні. *Підприємництво, господарство і право*. 2017. № 5. С. 151–155.

Нооркиїв Р. Як адміністративна реформа в Естонії підсилює місцеве самоврядування. *Децентралізація: Офіційний вебпортал*. 2021. URL: https://decentralization. gov.ua/news/13820#_ftn14

Обласна програма розвитку міжнародного співробітництва на 2022–2024 рр. *Рівненська обласна державна адміністрація:* Офіційний вебсайт. URL: https://www. rv.gov.ua/pro-oblasnu-programu-rozvitku-mizhnarodnogo-spivrobitnictva-na-2022-2024-roki-proekt

Оболенський О. Державне управління та державна служба: словник-довідник. Київ: КНЕУ, 2005. 311 с.

Одінцова Г. Державне управління і менеджмент. Харків: ХарРІ НАДУ, 2002. 492 с.

Онищук І. Аналіз виконання місцевих бюджетів за 2022 рік. *Децентралізація: Офіційний вебпортал*. URL:https://decentralization.gov.ua/news/16105

Організація співробітництва територіальних громад в Україні: практичний посібник для посадових осіб місцевого самоврядування. Київ, 2017. 105 с. URL: https://decentralization.gov.ua/uploads/library/file/11/Organizatsiya-spivrobitnitstva-teritorialnih-gromad-v-Ukrayini.pdf

Оржель О., Палій. О. Європейський досвід державного управління: курс лекцій. Київ: Вид-во НАДУ, 2007. 76 с.

Оффердал О. Политика и проблемы организационного дизайна в местном самоуправлении. *Полис*. 1988. № 1. С. 52–67.

Оцінка громадянами України наслідків реформи децентралізації і готовність брати участь у житті місцевої громади. Бачення ролі бізнесу в розвитку громад (травень 2021 р.). *Центр Разумкова*.URL: https://razumkov.org.ua/napriamky/ sotsiologichni-doslidzhennia/otsinka-gromadianamy-ukrainy-naslidkiv-reformy-detsentralizatsii-i-gotovnist-braty-uchast-u-zhytti-mistsevoi-gromady-bachennia-roli-biznesu-v-rozvytku-gromad-traven-2021r

Падалко В. Централізація та децентралізація в організації служби в органах місцевого самоврядування: муніципально-правовий аспект. *Держава і право*. 2012. № 57. С. 123–129.

Панейко Ю. Теоретичні основи самоврядування. Львів: Літопис, 2002. 196 с.

Парламент підтримав законопроєкт щодо функціонування місцевого самоврядування під час воєнного стану. *Міністерство розвитку громад та тери-*

торій України: Офіційний вебсайт. URL: https://www.minregion.gov.ua/press/ news/parlament-pidtrymav-zakonoproyekt-shhodo-funkczionuvannya-misczevogo-samovryaduvannya-pid-chas-voyennogo-stanu/

Пасько Я. Соціологія міста. Донецьк: Ноуліжд, 2010. 40 с.

Пиренн А. Средневековые города и возрождение торговли. Горький: Изд. Горьковского пед. ин-та, 1941. 125 с.

План реалізації Стратегії розвитку Білокуракинської об'єднаної територіальної громади 2020–2022 рр. *Білокуракинська громада:* Офіційний вебсайт. 2022. URL: https://bilokurakynska-gromada.gov.ua/strategichnij-plan-stalogo-rozvitku-bilokurakinskoi-selischnoi-teritorialnoi-gromadi-do-2026-roku-13-54-37-09-12-2016/

Понад 150 міст у світі вже розірвали відносини з російськими містами-побратимами. *Децентралізація:* Офіційний вебпортал.2022. URL: https://decentralization. gov.ua/news/14999

Понад півтори тисячі тонн гуманітарної допомоги відправили до різних регіонів України з Чернівців. *АрміяInform.* 2022. URL: https://armyinform.com. ua/2022/03/17/ponad-pivtory-tysyachi-tonn-gumanitarnoyi-dopomogy-vidpravyly-do-riznyh-regioniv-ukrayiny-z-chernivcziv/

*Портал Децентралізація.*URL: https://decentralization.gov.ua/

Порядок вирішення питань адміністративно-територіального устрою: законопроект йде на повторне перше читання. *Децентралізація:* Офіційний вебпортал. 2022. URL: https://decentralization.gov.ua/news/14574

Порядок денний асоціації між Україною та ЄС для підготовки та сприяння імплементації Угоди про асоціацію. *Урядовий портал.*URL: https://www.kmu.gov.ua/ storage/app/imported_content/news/doc_248012532/UA_15-1%20final.pdf

Постанова Кабінету Міністрів України «Про затвердження Державної стратегії регіонального розвитку на період до 2015 р.». *Верховна Рада України*: Офіційний вебсайт. URL: https://zakon.rada.gov.ua/laws/show/1001-2006-%D0%BF/page2

Постанова Кабінету міністрів України «Про затвердження Державної стратегії регіонального розвитку на 2021–2027 роки» від 5.08.2020 р. *Верховна Рада України:* Офіційний вебпортал. URL: https://zakon.rada.gov.ua/laws/show/695-2020-%D0%BF#Text

Постанова Центральної виборчої комісії «Про перші вибори депутатів сільських, селищних, міської рад об'єднаних територіальних громад і відповідних сільських, селищних, міського голів 22 грудня 2019 року» від 11.10.2019 р. *Центральна виборча комісія:* Офіційний вебпортал. URL: https://act.cvk.gov.ua/acts/ pro-pershi-vibori-deputativ-silskih-selishhnihmiskoi-rad-ob-iednanih-teritorialnih-gromad-i-vidpovidnih-silskih-selishhnihmiskogo-goliv-22-grudnya-2019-roku.html

Про кількість та склад населення України за підсумками. Всеукраїнського перепису населення 2001 року. *Державний комітет статистики України:* Офіційний вебсайт. URL: http://2001.ukrcensus.gov.ua/results/general/ nationality/

Про Стратегію сталого розвитку «Україна – 2020». Указ Президента України від 12.01.2015 р. № 5/2015. *Законодавство України.* URL: http://zakon4.rada.gov.ua/ laws/show/5/2015

Про схвалення Концепції реформування місцевого самоврядування та територіальної організації влади в Україні від 01.04.2014 р. *Законодавство України.* URL: https://zakon.rada.gov.ua/laws/show/333-2014-%D1%80#Text

Про схвалення проекту регіональної цільової програми розвитку міжнародного співробітництва та промоції Івано-Франківської області на 2022–2026 роки: *Розпорядження ОДА.* Офіційний вебсайт Івано-Франківської обласної державної адміністрації. URL: https://www.if.gov.ua/npas/pro-shvalennya-proektu-regionalnoyi-cilovoyi-programi-rozvitku-mizhnarodnogo-spivrobitnictva-ta-promociyi-ivano-frankivskoyi-oblasti-na-2022-2026-roki

Проблеми перерозподілу повноважень між районним та базовим рівнями місцевого самоврядування в сучасних умовах: аналітична записка. *Національний інститут стратегічних досліджень.* 2021. URL: https://niss.gov.ua/sites/default/files/2021-08/pererozpodil-povnovazen.pdf

Проблеми фінансування райрад. «Мінрегіон пропонував запровадити на перехідному етапі субвенцію районним бюджетам», – Олексій Чернишов. *Децентралізація: Офіційний вебпортал.* URL: https://decentralization.gov.ua/news/13528

Програма економічного і соціального розвитку Івано-Франківської міської територіальної громади на 2021–2023 роки. Офіційний сайт міста Івано-Франківська. 2022. URL: https://www.mvk.if.ua/sektors/54608

Проект Закону про внесення змін до Конституції України (щодо децентралізації влади) № 2217а від 01.07.2015 р. *Законодавство України.* URL: http://w1.c1.rada.gov.ua/pls/zweb2/webproc4_1?pf3511=55812

Проект Закону про місцевий референдум від 21.05.2021 р. *Верховна Рада України:* Офіційний вебпортал. URL: http://w1.c1.rada.gov.ua/pls/ zweb2/webproc4_1?pf3511=71942

Проект Закону про порядок вирішення питань адміністративно-територіального устрою України від 28.01.2021 р. *Верховна Рада України:* Офіційний вебсайт. URL: https://w1.c1.rada.gov.ua/pls/zweb2/webproc4_1? pf3511=70936

Проект Стратегії розвитку Прилісненської ОТГ 2021–2027 рр. *Прилісненська громада:* Офіційний вебсайт. URL: https://prylisnenska-gromada.gov.ua/strategichnij-plan-rozvitku-prilisnenskoi-teritorialnoi-goromadi-15-26-01-24-06-2020/

Проєкт Закону України «Про внесення змін до Закону України «Про місцеве самоврядування в Україні» щодо комунальної власності». *Міністерство розвитку громад та територій України:* Офіційний вебсайт. URL: https://www.minregion.gov.ua/base-law/grom-convers/elektronni-konsultatsiyi-z-gromadskistyu/proekt-zakonu-ukrayiny-pro-vnesennya-zmin-do-zakonu-ukrayiny-pro-misczeve-samovryaduvannya-v-ukrayini-shhodo-komunalnoyi-vlasnosti/

Проєкт Стратегії сталого розвитку Нетішинської міської об'єднаної територіальної громади на період до 2028 р. *Нетішинська міська рада:* Офіційний вебсайт. URL: https://www.netishynrada.gov.ua/DOC/publ-inf/%D0%A1%D2%D0%A0%D0%90%D0%A2%D0%95%D0%93I%D0%AF_%D0%9D%D0%B5%D1%82%D1%96%D1%88%D0%B8%D0%BD%D1%81%D1%8C%D0%BA%D0%B0-%D0%9E%D0%A2%D0%93-%D0%B4%D0%BE-2028.docx

Проєкт Стратегії сталого розвитку Солонківської сільської об'єднаної територіальної громади на 2019–2027 рр. (нова редакція). *Солонківська територі-*

альна громада: Офіційний вебсайт. URL: https://solonkivska-gromada.gov.ua/strategichne-planuvannya-14-42-01-13-09-2018/

Протокол № 3 до Європейської рамкової конвенції про транскордонне співробітництво між територіальними общинами або властями стосовно об'єднань єврорегіонального співробітництва. *Верховна Рада України:* Офіційний вебсайт. URL: https://zakon.rada.gov.ua/laws/show/994_947#Text

Прямі іноземні інвестиції в регіони України. *VoxUkraine.* 2022. URL: https://voxukraine.org/pryami-inozemni-investytsiyi-v-regiony-ukrayiny/

Рада ухвалила закон для завершення децентралізації. *Укрінформ.* 17 листопада 2020 р. URL: https://www.ukrinform.ua/rubric-polytics/3137893-rada-uhvalila-zakon-pro-reorganizaciu-gromad-i-rajoniv.html

Регіональна програма розвитку міжнародного співробітництва Чернівецької області на 2021–2023 роки. *Чернівецька обласна державна адміністрація:* Офіційний вебсайт. URL: https://bukoda.gov.ua/storage/app/sites/23/Prohramy/dep%20comm/rehionalna-prohrama-rozvytku-mizhnarodnoho-spivrobitnytstva-chernivetskoyi-oblasti-na-2021-2023-roky.pdf

Регульський Є. У реформи місцевого самоврядування буде багато ворогів. *Лівий берег.* 2014. URL: https://lb.ua/society/2014/07/15/272846_lektsiya.html

Реєстр договорів про співробітництво територіальних громад. *Міністерство розвитку громад та територій України:* Офіційний вебсайт. URL: https://www.minregion.gov.ua/napryamki-diyalnosti/rozvytok-mistsevoho-samovryaduvannya/reyestr/

Реєстр міжрегіональних угод про торговельно-економічне, науково-технічне і культурне співробітництво. *Міністерство розвитку громад та територій України*: Офіційний вебсайт. URL: https://www.minregion.gov.ua/napryamki-diyalnosti/derzhavna-rehional-na-polityka/mizhregionalne-ta-transkordonne-spivrobitnitstv/reyestr-mizhregionalnih-ugod-pro-torgovelno-ekonomichne-naukovo-tehnichne-i-kulturne-spivrobitnitstvo/

Рівень довіри до суспільних інститутів та електоральні орієнтації громадян України (2019 р., 2021 р.). *Центр Разумкова.*URL: https://razumkov.org.ua/

Розпорядження Кабінету міністрів України «Про схвалення Концепції реформування місцевого самоврядування та територіальної організації влади в Україні» від 1.04.2014 р. *Верховна Рада України:* Офіційний вебресурс. URL: https://zakon.rada.gov.ua/laws/show/333-2014-%D1%80#Text

Романюк А. Методологічні основи виборчих досліджень. Теоретичні та практичні аспекти проведення виборчих кампаній. *Сучасні методи та інструменти політичної науки: колективна монографія (за результатами серії теоретичних і практичних воркшопів у рамках проекту «Удосконалення методів та інструментів політології в Україні: вплив університетів країн Вишеградської четвірки» від 13–15 вересня 2019 року).* Львів: Львівський національний університет імені Івана Франка, 2020. С. 182–212.

Романюк А. Національні та регіональні політичні процеси: визначення та виміри. *Теоретико-методологічні підходи до вивчення суспільно-політичних інститутів та процесів: колективна монографія.* Ужгород: Поліграфцентр «Ліра», 2022. С. 179–200.

Романюк А. Особливості та тенденції трансформації членської бази в політичних партіях України. *Вісник Львівського університету. Серія «Філософсько-політологічні студії».* 2022. № 43. С. 295–305.

Савчин М. (у співавт.). *Упровадження децентралізації публічної влади в Україні: національний і міжнародний аспекти.* Ужгород: TIMPANI, 2015. 216 с.

Саєнко П. Теоретичні засади формування стратегії розвитку об'єднаної територіальної громади. *Економіка і суспільство.* 2016. № 7. С. 594–598.

Самоврядування та децентралізацію вже можна викладати у школі. *Децентралізація*: Офіційний вебпортал. 2020. URL: https://decentralization.gov.ua/news/12853

Сванидзе А. Генезис феодального города в раннесредневековой Европе: проблемы и типология. *Городская жизнь в средневековой Европе.* Москва: Знание, 1987. С. 7–114.

Серьогіна С. Державне будівництво і місцеве самоврядування в Україні. Харків: Право, 2005. 256 с.

Сірік З. Проблеми та можливості співробітництва територіальних громад України. *Інвестиції: практика та досвід.* 2017. № 16. С. 102–107.

Скрипнюк О. Децентралізація влади як чинник забезпечення стабільності конституційного ладу: теорія й практика. *Віче.* 2015. № 12. С. 22–24.

Стратегічний план розвитку Калинівської міської об'єднаної територіальної громади на 2020–2030 роки. *Калинівська міська рада:* Офіційний вебсайт. 2022. URL: https://kalynivska-objednana-gromada.gov.ua/strategiya-rozvitku-14-41-19-12-06-2019/

Стратегічний план розвитку Кам'янської міської об'єднаної територіальної громади на період 2019–2028 рр. *Кам'янська міська рада:* Офіційний вебсайт. URL: https://kammiskrada.gov.ua/wp-content/uploads.pdf

Стратегія розвитку Бахмутської міської ОТГ на період до 2027 р. *Офіційний сайт Бахмутської міської ради.* 2022. URL: https://drive.google.com/file/d/15BdOvhZu4paFporD5-_Lrl6JhGekmnWp/view

Стратегія розвитку Березнегуватської селищної ради на період до 2027 р. *Березнегуватська громада:* Офіційний вебсайт. URL: https://berezneguvatska-gromada.gov.ua/strategii-rozvitku-berezneguvatskoi-ob%E2%80%99ednanoi-teritorialno-gromadi-11-53-13-22-02-2021

Стратегія розвитку Вчорайшенської сільської об'єднаної територіальної громади до 2027 р. *Вчорайшенська громада*: Офіційний вебсайт. URL: https://vchorayshenska-gromada.gov.ua/docs/461791/

Стратегія розвитку Гребінківської міської об'єднаної територіальної громади до 2028 р. Гребінківська міська об'єднана територіальна громада: Офіційний вебсайт. 2022. URL: http://www.hrebinka.org.ua/data/files/new/strategiya/strateg_final2.pdf

Стратегія розвитку Музиківської об'єднаної громади на 2017–2025 рр.URL: https://muzykivskaotg.gov.ua/storage/documents/attachments/163c3b8f03f39eff26d796f94413b6c4.pdf

Стратегія розвитку Мукачівської міської об'єднаної територіальної громади до 2027 року. *Мукачівська міська рада:* Офіційний вебсайт. 2022. URL: https://

mukachevo-rada.gov.ua/upravlinnya-mistom/strategiya-2027/strategiya-rozvitku-mukachivskoyi-otg-do-2027-roku

Стратегія розвитку Набутівської ОТГ на період до 2025 р. *Набутівська громада*: Офіційний вебсайт. 2022. URL: https://nabutivska-gromada.gov.ua/strategiya-rozvitku-nabutivskoi-otg-na-period-do-2025-roku-08-38-31-30-01-2018/

Стратегія розвитку Недригайлівської об'єднаної територіальної громади на 2018–2025 рр. *Недригайлівська громада*: Офіційний вебсайт. URL: https://nedrygaylivska-gromada.gov.ua/strategiya-rozvitku-nedrigajlivskoi-ob%E2%80%99ednanoi-teritorialnoi-gromadi-na-20182025-rr-08-11-54-30-10-2018/

Стратегія розвитку Нововодолазької селищної територіальної громади на 2018–2025 рр. (нова редакція). URL: https://vodolaga-gromada.gov.ua/storage/economic-profile/general/84beb608750e001e76590b70bebff346.pdf

Стратегія розвитку Новопразької селищної об'єднаної територіальної громади. 2019. URL: https://rada.info/upload/users_files/04366086/d5dcdb3f1214ad87253b2b 47c4fb1d5d.pdf

Стратегія розвитку Обухівської міської територіальної громади Київської області на 2022–2027 роки. *Обухівська міська рада:* Офіційний вебсайт. 2022. URL: https://obcity.gov.ua/gromadyanam/ekonomika-mista/strategiya-rozvitku/

Стратегія розвитку Преображенської сільської об'єднаної територіальної громади на 2021–2027 рр. *Преображенська об'єднана територіальна громада:* Офіційний вебсайт. URL: https://preobrazhenska-gromada.gov.ua/plan-zahodiv-na-20212023-roki-z-realizacii-strategii-rozvitku-preobrazhenskoi-silskoi-ob%E2%80%99ednanoi-teritorialnoi-gromadi-na-20212027-roki-1600251247/

Стратегія розвитку Рівненської територіальної громади на період до 2027 р. *Рівненська міська рада:* Офіційний вебсайт. URL: http://rivnerada.gov.ua/portal-files/portal/.pdf

Стратегія розвитку Сновської міської територіальної громади на 2021–2027 рр. *Сновська міська рада:* Офіційний вебсайт. URL: https://snovmr.gov.ua/pro-zatverdzhennya-strategiyi-rozvytku-snovskoyi-miskoyi-terytorialnoyi-gromady-na-2021-2027-roky/

Стратегія розвитку Шабівської об'єднаної територіальної громади Білгород-Дністровського району Одеської області на 2019–2030 рр. *Шабівська сільська рада об'єднана територіальна громада:* Офіційний вебсайт. 2022. URL: https://shabivska-gromada.gov.ua/strategiya-rozvitku-shabivskoi-otg-15-39-52-05-03-2019/

Стратегія сталого розвитку Великогаївської сільської об'єднаної територіальної громади на 2018–2025 рр. *Великогаївська громада:* Офіційний вебсайт. URL: https://velykogaivska-gromada.gov.ua/starategiya-rozvitku-gromadi-12-01-47-07-02-2017/

Стратегія сталого розвитку Хотинської територіальної громади на 2021–2027 рр. URL: https://khotyn.dosvit.org.ua/storage/documents/ documents/23361df827027b34 034d62878ba33e1d.pdf

Суспільно-політичні настрої населення України: опитування (24 липня – 1 серпня 2021 р.). *Київський міжнародний інститут соціології.* URL: https://www.kiis.com.ua/?lang=ukr&cat=reports&id=1055&page=1 Тараненко Г. Досвід децентралізації у країнах ЄС. *Інструменти і практики публічного управління в контексті* децентралізації: матеріали ІІ Всеукраїнської науково-практичної конференції за міжнародною участю (23 червня 2020 року). Житомир: Поліський національний університет, 2020. С. 131–136.

Тарасенко Н. Особливості підготовки та проведення місцевих виборів-2020 в оцінках експертів. *Україна: події, факти, коментарі*. 2020. № 10. URL: http://nbuviap.gov.ua/images/ukraine/2020/ukr10.pdf.

Тимченко І. Територіальна громада у транскордонному просторі: чинники, закономірності, пріоритети розвитку: монографія. Львів: ДУ «Інститут регіональних досліджень імені М. І. Долішнього НАН України», 2019. 444 с.

Токвіль А. Про демократію в Америці. Київ: Видавничий дім «Всесвіт», 1999. 590 с.

Тьерри О. Исчезновение античного рабства (Смешение рас). Санкт-Петербург: [s.n.], 1912. 505 с.

У Києва стало більше міст-побратимів: Кличко зустрівся з мерами 8 європейських міст. *LB.ua*. 2022. URL: https://lb.ua/news/2022/08/20/526840_klichko_zustrivsya_z_merami_8.html

Угода між Міністерством територіального планування і будівництва Республіки Польща та Державним комітетом України у справах містобудування і архітектури про утворення польсько-української Комісії з територіального планування від 25.06.1996 р. *Верховна Рада України*: Офіційний вебсайт. URL: https://zakon.rada.gov.ua/laws/show/616_047#Text

Угода між Урядом України та Урядом Республіки Польща від 24.05.1993 р. *Верховна Рада України:* Офіційний вебсайт. URL: https://zakon.rada.gov.ua/laws/show/616_171#Text

Угода про асоціацію між Україною, з однієї сторони, та Європейським Союзом, Європейським співтовариством з атомної енергії і їхніми державами-членами, з іншої сторони. *Законодавство України*. URL: https://zakon.rada.gov.ua/laws/show/984_011#Text

Угорщина виділяє майже 6 мільйонів євро на виплати «постраждалим від війни» угорцям Закарпаття. *InfoPost.Media*. 2022. URL: https://infopost.media/ugorshhyna-vydilyaye-majzhe-6-miljoniv-yevro-na-vyplaty-postrazhdalym-vid-vijny-ugorczyam-zakarpattya/

Угорщина передала на Закарпаття перший гумантаж. *Укрінформ*. 2022. URL: https://www.ukrinform.ua/rubric-regions/3415011-ugorsina-peredala-na-zakarpatta-persij-gumvantaz.html

Узун Ю. Чинник концепції «Європа регіонів» в процесах децентралізації в Україні. *Вісник ОНУ ім. І. І. Мечникова. Соціологія і політичні науки*. 2018. Т. 23. №2 (31). С. 162–179.

Указ Президента України «Про Концепцію державної регіональної політики» від 25.05.2001 р. *Верховна Рада України:* Офіційний вебресурс. URL: https://zakon.rada.gov.ua/laws/show/341/2001#Text

Українським громадам допомагають європейські міста-побратими. *Асоціація міст України:* Офіційний вебсайт. 2022. URL: https://auc.org.ua/novyna/ukrayinskym-gromadam-dopomagayut-yevropeyski-mista-pobratymy

Українці довіряють місцевій владі більше, ніж центральній – дослідження «Active Group». *Асоціація міст України:* Офіційний вебсайт. 2020. URL: https://auc.org.ua/novyna/ukrayinci-doviryayut-misceviy-vladi-bilshe-nizh-centralniy-doslidzhennya-active-group

Улютін Д. Бюджетна децентралізація: головні виклики та досягнення. *Децентралізація:* Офіційний вебпортал. 2020. URL: https://decentralization.gov.ua/news/12661

Урядовий законопроєкт про адмінтерустрій усуває громади від управління своїми територіями, – АМУ. *Асоціація міст України.* 2022. URL: https://www.auc.org.ua/novyna/uryadovyy-zakonoproyekt-pro-adminterustriy-usuvaye-gromady-vid-upravlinnya-svoyimy

Федоренко В., Чернеженко О. Конституційні моделі місцевого самоврядування у державах-учасницях ЄС, Швейцарії та Україні: монографія. Київ: Ліра-К, 2017. 288 с.

Хорт І. Методологічні проблеми дослідження функцій місцевого самоврядування. Віче. 2015. № 12. URL: https://veche.kiev.ua/journal/4781/

Центральна виборча комісія: Офіційний вебсайт. URL: https://www.cvk.gov.ua/vibory_category/mistsevi-vibori/vibori-deputativ-verhovnoi-radi-avtonomnoi-respubliki-krim-oblasnih-rayonnih-miskih-rayonnih-silskih-selishhnih-rad-25-10-2020.html#

Цірнер М., Марадик Н. Особливості фіскальної децентралізації в Словацькій Республіці: досвід для України. *Політичне життя.* 2020. № 2. С. 57–62.

Чернеженко О. Конституційні основи місцевого самоврядування в державах-учасницях Європейського Союзу і в Україні. Дис. на здобуття наук. ст. д.ю.н. Київ: Національна академія внутрішніх справ, 2019. 521 с.

Чернишов О. Наша наступна мета – створити у громадах додатково 350 Центрів безпеки. *Децентралізація:* Офіційний вебпортал. URL: https://decentralization.gov.ua/news/14187

Чому децентралізація політичної влади в Україні є завданням європейської інтеграції? *Євроінтеграційний портал.* URL: https://eu-ua.kmu.gov.ua/analityka/chomu-decentralizaciya-politychnoyi-vlady-v-ukrayini-ye-zavdannyam-yevropeyskoyi

Чудик Н. Історія статутів територіальних громад. *Науковий вісник Ужгородського національного університету. Серія «Право».* 2013. № 22. С. 122–124.

Шведський погляд на нагляд у місцевому самоврядуванні. *Децентралізація: Офіційний вебпортал.* 2020. URL: https://decentralization.gov.ua/news/12460

Шумовська К. Методологія дослідження місцевого самоврядування. *Державне управління: удосконалення та розвиток.* 2011. № 12. URL: http://www.dy.nayka.com.ua/?op=1&z=384

Щедрова Г. Інституційна пам'ять: концептуалізація в політологічному дискурсі. *Політикус.* 2021. № 5. С. 17–22.

Щербатюк О. Дефініція «інвестиційний потенціал підприємства»: сутність та відмінності. *Ефективна економіка.* 2011. № 11. URL: http://www.economy.nayka.com.ua/?op=1&z=773.

Як відбувалися вибори Президента України з часів незалежності. *Суспільне мовлення*. 2019. URL: https://pl.suspilne.media/news/19451

Як міста-побратими можуть допомогти у відновленні України? Приклади та інструкція. *Рубрика*. 2022. URL: https://rubryka.com/article/twin-cities-help-ukraine/

www.ingramcontent.com/pod-product-compliance
Lightning Source LLC
Chambersburg PA
CBHW070346270326
41926CB00017B/4011